PETERSON'S

Game Plan for Getting into Graduate School

Marion B. Castellucci

Peterson's
Thomson Learning™

Australia • Canada • Denmark • Japan • Mexico
New Zealand • Philippines • Puerto Rico • Singapore
Spain • United Kingdom • United States

About Peterson's

Founded in 1966, Peterson's, a division of Thomson Learning, is the nation's largest and most respected provider of lifelong learning online resources, software, reference guides, and books. The Education Supersite^{SM} at petersons.com—the Web's most heavily traveled education resource—has searchable databases and interactive tools for contacting U.S.-accredited institutions and programs. CollegeQuest^{SM} (CollegeQuest.com) offers a complete solution for every step of the college decision-making process. GradAdvantage^{TM} (GradAdvantage.org), developed with Educational Testing Service, is the only electronic admissions service capable of sending official graduate test score reports with a candidate's online application. Peterson's serves over 55 million education consumers annually.

Thomson Learning is among the world's largest providers of lifelong learning information. Headquartered in Stamford, CT, with multiple offices worldwide, Thomson Learning is a division of The Thomson Corporation (TTC), one of the world's leading information companies. TTC operates mainly in the U.S., Canada, and the UK and has annual revenues of over US$6 billion. The Corporation's common shares are traded on the Toronto, Montreal, and London stock exchanges. For more information, visit TTC's Internet address at www.thomcorp.com.

Visit Peterson's Education Center on the Internet (World Wide Web) at www.petersons.com

ISBN 0-7689-0391-2

Printed in Canada

10   9   8   7   6   5   4   3   2   1

I'd like to thank the many faculty members and administrators who generously shared their knowledge of graduate education, offered suggestions on how applicants can improve their chances of admission to graduate school, and put me in touch with their students. Among them are Gail Ashley, Rutgers University; David Faust, University of Rhode Island; Gladys M. Fleckles, California State University at Fullerton; Ed Goldberg, SetonWorldWide, Seton Hall University; Janelle Heineke, Graduate School of Management, Boston University; David S. Holmes, University of Kansas at Lawrence; Martha J. Johnson, Virginia Polytechnic Institute and State University (Virginia Tech); Emerelle McNair, Southern Polytechnic State University, Georgia; Richard Olivo, Harvard University; Jeanne Reesman, University of Texas at San Antonio; Jonathan Roberts, Pepperdine University; Thomas R. Rochon, Claremont Graduate University; Teresa M. Shaw, Claremont Graduate University; Donna Lau Smith, Cox School of Business, Southern Methodist University; Jay Sokolovsky, University of South Florida; Rose Ann Trantham, University of Tennessee at Knoxville; Suzette Vandeburg, State University of New York at Binghamton; Maria Vesperi, New College, State University of Florida; and J. W. Viers, Virginia Tech.

To the present and former students who took time out from their hectic schedules to educate me about the realities of graduate school, many, many thanks: Felecia Bartow, Washington University in St. Louis; Brenda Bennett, Cambridge College; Cathryn A. Chappell, University of Cincinnati; Jennifer Cheavens, University of Kansas at Lawrence; Robert J. Connelly, Seton Hall University; Luis De la Cruz, Worcester Polytechnic Institute; Kimberly A. Foreman, SetonWorldWide, Seton Hall University; Thomas J. Fuchs, California Institute of Professional Psychology; Carol Jean Godby, Ohio State University; Tammy Lynn Hammershoy, Western Connecticut State University; Heather Helms-Erikson, Pennsylvania State University; Melany Kahn, New York University; Matthew J. Kinkley, University of Toledo; Neill

Acknowledgments

Acknowledgments

A. Kipp, Virginia Tech; Renee Vaillantcourt Lantz, Worcester Polytechnic Institute; James M. Lipuma, New Jersey Institute of Technology; Cynthia M. Liutkus, Rutgers University; Joyce May, University of Rhode Island; Megan McAfee, Virginia Tech; Nestor Montilla, John Jay College of Criminal Justice; Stephanie Muntone, New York University; Andrea Edwards Myers, The College of St. Rose; Leslie Nelman, Monterey Institute of International Studies; Laurie R. Noe, Nova Southeastern University; Michael Ogburn, Virginia Tech; Naaz Qureshi, Cox School of Business, Southern Methodist University; Jesse Sokolovsky, Vassar College; Daniel J. Stollenwerk, Pontifical Institute of Salamanca; Kimberly Tremblay, Harvard University; Kimani C. Toussaint, Jr., Boston University; Jennifer Wagaman, University of Alaska at Fairbanks; David A. Watkins, Virginia Tech; and those who wished to remain nameless.

Finally, I'd like to express my deep appreciation to my friend Denise A. Kaiser, M.A., University of Toronto, and Ph.D., Columbia University, for reading the manuscript in draft and offering many excellent suggestions for its improvement.

Marion B. Castellucci

Contents

Introduction

So, you are thinking about going to graduate school. Perhaps you are a junior or senior in college and you want to do advanced work in a subject you love. Perhaps you'd like to enter a profession, like law, medicine, or social work, that requires specialized training as one of the prerequisites for employment.

Or maybe, if you are like many people pursuing graduate education today, your college years are behind you. You have been working for a couple of years (or decades) and your career has reached the point at which it needs a boost from further education. Perhaps you need to return to school to keep up with advances in your field. Or you want to switch careers entirely, and to do so, you need a degree in your new field. Or, you simply need a new intellectual challenge to broaden your horizons.

Whatever your reasons for considering graduate school, you should think carefully before taking this step. Going to graduate school because you're not sure what else to do is not a good idea. Graduate school is a huge investment of your time and money. The key is to be sure of what you want to get out of your education before you make that investment. If you invest wisely, your graduate education can enrich your life intellectually, professionally, and financially.

So, is graduate school right for you? To answer this question, you need to approach it from two directions. First, you are going to have to look inward and analyze your personal strengths, weaknesses, situation, and goals. Then, you are going to have to do a lot of research to find graduate programs that suit you and that will help you achieve your goals. This book will help you start both processes.

AN OVERVIEW OF GRADUATE EDUCATION

Degree Programs

Traditionally, graduate education has been either academic or professional in orientation. Academic graduate education emphasizes performing and evaluating research. For example, a graduate student in

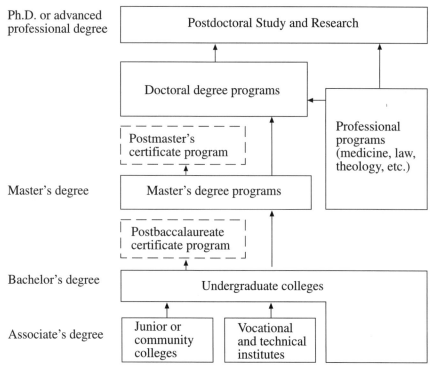

Structure of postsecondary education in the United States. Note that the arrows indicate common pathways of students, but not the only possible pathways.

Source: Adapted from U.S. Department of Education, National Center for Educational Statistics.

experimental psychology may conduct research on the relationship between aerobic exercise and stress. On the other hand, professional graduate education emphasizes learning the skills and knowledge necessary to practice a profession. So, for example, the emphasis of a graduate student in clinical psychology may be to learn how to provide psychotherapy.

Graduate education in an academic field, like history, English literature, or biochemistry involves acquiring, evaluating, and communicating knowledge in a narrow aspect of a broad subject. The first postbaccalaureate academic degree is the Master of Arts (M.A.) or Master of Science (M.S.). To earn such a degree, the student takes courses and engages in research, whether in the library, the laboratory, or in the field. For some master's degrees, the student must also write a master's thesis. An academic master's degree may qualify you to go on to doctoral study, or it may simply improve your attractiveness to employers. Many employers consider a master's degree an indicator of good research, critical-thinking, and communication skills. A master's degree takes a year or two to earn on a full-time basis.

The highest academic degree, the Doctor of Philosophy (Ph.D.), requires further course work beyond the master's level as well as original, specialized research culminating in a dissertation. For example, Denise Kaiser, who earned a Ph.D. in medieval history, has a broad knowledge of this time period from courses she has taken. From researching and writing her dissertation, she also has specialized knowledge of a small aspect of the subject: what thirteenth century sermons can tell us about the education of the preacher and the concerns of his audience. Because there is so much work involved, earning a Ph.D. can take from four to ten years. People who earn academic Ph.D.'s usually hope to do research and/or teach at the university level.

> **People who earn academic Ph.D.'s usually hope to do research and/or teach at the university level.**

In contrast to academic graduate education, professional education emphasizes the practical application of knowledge and skills. For some professions, a master's degree may be preferred or even required for employment. For example, social workers need a Master of Social Work (M.S.W.) and librarians need a Master of Library Science (M.L.S.). In other professions, one of the prerequisites is a doctoral degree. To practice medicine, for example, you need a Doctor of Medicine degree (M.D.); to become an optometrist, a Doctor of Optometry degree (O.D.). But in many fields, professional master's degrees and doctoral degrees are optional. People who pursue them do so to advance their careers. Degrees in business administration, journalism, fine arts, and environmental science, for example, are not required for employment but may help people find work and prosper in these fields.

To further complicate the picture, the distinction between academic and professional graduate education is beginning to blur. Some academic programs, faced with poor employment prospects in academia for their Ph.D.'s, have begun to integrate aspects of professional education in order to make their students more marketable. Some now require students to do internships to gain practical experience in related fields. For example, at the University of Texas in Dallas, doctoral students in chemistry take courses for three semesters, then intern in a chemicals firm for three semesters, and finally return to campus to write a thesis.

Many institutions now offer combined degree programs in which students can study both professional and academic subjects. Boston College, for example, offers a combined degree program in business administration and Russian and Eastern European studies (M.B.A./M.A.), while Arizona State offers a combined degree in anthropology and justice studies (M.A./M.S.). At many institutions, you can design your own combined degree program tailored to your academic and professional interests. At New York University, Stephanie Muntone combined an M.A. in history with a certificate in archival management.

Finally, a rapidly growing type of graduate education is the certificate program. Certificate programs are usually aimed at working professionals who seek to upgrade job skills or meet the requirements of a professional credentialing body or a master's program. To serve these students, certificate programs are offered part-time and they are short, typically 18 hours for a postbaccalaureate certificate and 24 hours for a postmaster's certificate. Almost half of all certificates are granted in the field of education. Most of these fulfill state requirements for elementary or secondary teaching. Other popular fields are health sciences, particularly in areas of interest to nurse practitioners, and social sciences, mainly in psychology and counseling. Finally, some certificate programs are offered in the arts and sciences, including area and ethnic studies, and they are often interdisciplinary. One of the most popular of these is the women's studies certificate.

> Popular fields for certificate programs are education, health sciences, and women's studies.

Institutions

Degrees through the doctorate level are generally offered at universities, both public and private. Some universities are research universities and others are teaching universities. What's the difference? Funding, for one thing. Large research universities receive money—often millions of dollars a year—from the federal government and private sources to support the research efforts of their faculties. In these institutions, graduate education focuses on preparing students for a career in academic, field, or laboratory research. At teaching universities, the emphasis is on preparing you for a career in teaching at the college level. Many universities combine the features of both research and teaching institutions.

Many universities also offer professional degrees from their professional schools. In addition to a school of arts and sciences, a university may also have schools of medicine, law, journalism, education, engineering, and social work, to name a few. These usually offer master's degrees and doctoral degrees. Master's degrees are also offered by some colleges as well as universities.

To accommodate the wide variety of students now seeking graduate education, some institutions have developed innovative alternatives to traditional courses of study. Although many programs, especially the traditional academic ones, still require full-time enrollment and your presence on campus, many others do not. Some programs offer part-time enrollment, allowing you to work full—time and take longer to complete the requirements for a degree. Others have established satellite locations to make getting to classes easier if you live far from the main campus. And some have established distance learning programs, in which it doesn't really matter where you are. In these programs, most instruction and communication is achieved through telecommunications, with periodic face-to-face meetings. In fact, there is even a new type of institution—the virtual university, which operates primarily through telecommunications.

WHAT IS A GRADUATE DEGREE WORTH?

The value of a graduate degree is known only to the person who possesses it. It may be priceless if it has opened the door to a subject or work you love. Or it may be worthless if it's left you unemployed or underemployed in your field and disappointed in your vocation. This is the lot of many new academic Ph.D.'s who had their hearts set on a career in research and university-level teaching. Today, fewer than half of new academic Ph.D.'s find permanent employment in academia; instead, most are employed in government, business, or the nonprofit sector.

However, you *can* measure the worth of a graduate degree in earning power. The fact is that, on average, people with graduate degrees, especially professional degrees, make more money than people without graduate degrees, as you can see in the bar graph below. For many people, the desire to make more money is a prime motivation for acquiring a graduate degree. But before you leap to the conclusion that a graduate degree causes an automatic increase in salary, be aware that it may be that people who go to graduate school are simply more ambitious and driven than people who do not. These personality traits may contribute to their success in their careers as much as, or more than, the degree itself.

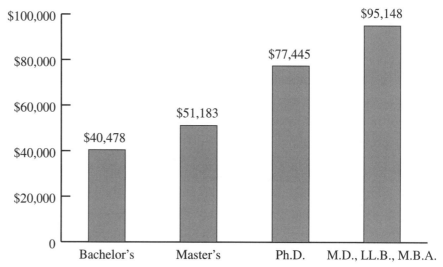

Average annual income, by highest degree attained.

Source: "Educational Attainment in the United States," U.S. Bureau of the Census, 1997.

One factor that contributes to the value of a graduate degree is its relative scarcity. If you look at the U.S. population as a whole, very few people have postbaccalaureate degrees. You can see from the circle graph, for example, that only 1 percent of Americans over age 25 have an academic doctoral degree. Only about 5 percent hold a master's degree.

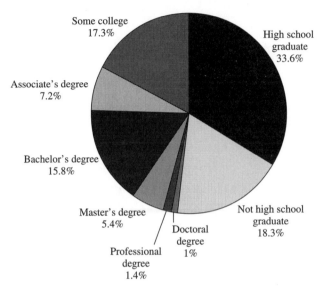

Highest level of educational attainment by people 25 years and older.

1996 Source: U.S. Department of Commerce, Bureau of the Census, Current Population Survey, unpublished data.

Comparing the value of a graduate degree with its cost is another way to evaluate whether graduate school is right for you. Like undergraduate tuition and fees, the cost of graduate education has been rising rapidly. You can easily spend more than $30,000 a year for a graduate program at a top private university. Tuition and fees at public institutions are much less, which probably helps account for the fact that about 70 percent of all graduate students attend public universities.

Much less financial aid is available for graduate studies as compared to undergraduate programs, and the amount of aid is decreasing. Thus, the amount of debt assumed by grad students is on the rise. In Chapter 8, we'll discuss the finances of graduate school in more detail and offer some suggestions for finding financial aid.

TRENDS IN GRADUATE EDUCATION

Enrollment

There may not be many people with graduate degrees, relatively speaking, but their numbers increased steadily from the early 1980's to the mid-1990's. During that period, both applications and enrollment increased, with much of the increase due to larger numbers of women and minority students. According to the Council of Graduate Schools, graduate applications began to decrease and enrollment started to level off in 1993. Since then there has been a slight downward trend in graduate enrollment among both men and women in all types of educational institutions and in almost all fields of study.

Why has this happened? The main reason is the strong labor market of the late 1990s. With the unemployment rate the lowest it had been since 1970, newly graduated B.A.'s found good job opportunities in almost all fields. In 1999 alone, the number of jobs available for people with B.A.'s was expected to increase by 10 percent, with a 4.8 percent increase in starting salary. In addition, press reports about an oversupply of Ph.D.'s have also discouraged potential applicants. Under these circumstances, it's hardly surprising that many college graduates decided to enter the labor market rather than go to graduate school during the 1990s. "None of my friends went to graduate school," says Jesse Sokolovsky, who graduated from Vassar College in 1999 with a degree in computer science. "They're all working for computer companies."

You may be thinking that this is good news for you—less competition for admission, right? Well, not exactly. Reduced federal funding for higher education has meant less money for public universities, fewer grants for professors, and fewer graduate fellowships. In the arts and sciences, many universities have downsized their programs, admitting fewer students. Thus, competition for admission to the top universities and professional schools and even the second-tier has increased. Still, if you approach finding and applying to graduate programs in a realistic, thorough manner, you should be able to find a program that meets your needs.

"None of my friends went to graduate school," says Jesse Sokolovsky, who graduated from Vassar College in 1999 with a degree in computer science. **"They're all working for computer companies."**

Who Goes to Grad School?

Today, nearly one quarter of all graduate students are over age 40, reflecting the trend toward lifelong learning. Whereas in the past people tended to pursue their graduate education in their 20s, today, rapid changes in technology and the workplace have propelled older workers back to school at various stages of their careers. Increases in the number of women and minorities pursuing graduate degrees accounted for most of the graduate school enrollment growth of the past few decades. For example, editor Andrea Edwards Myers had not taken a college course in twenty-five years when she decided to go back to school for a master's in public communications. "I was very out of practice," she says, "but I found that, due to my professional background, I bring a lot to the table and can contribute in class more than I thought I could at the beginning."

Of the approximately 1,200,000 people enrolled in U.S. graduate programs, more than half are women, more than one third are minority students, and about one tenth are international students. In fact, increases in the number of women and minorities pursuing graduate degrees accounted for most of the enrollment growth of the past few decades. The continued strong presence of women and minorities, along with that of foreign students, has kept enrollment figures from plummeting in the late 1990s. The chief uncertainty in this picture is the effect of California's Proposition 209 and similar government actions on future minority enrollment. Among other things, Proposition 209 outlawed preferential treatment on the basis of gender, race, and ethnicity for people applying to California state universities—effectively dismantling affirmative action programs that had helped level the playing field for women and members of minority groups. Proposition 209 is being challenged in the courts, so its long-term effect on enrollment, in California and elsewhere, is hard to predict.

> **Increases in the number of women and minorities pursuing graduate degrees accounted for most of the graduate school enrollment growth of the past few decades.**

Fields of Study

What are graduate students studying? By far, the largest group—almost one fifth of all students—are enrolled in graduate programs in education. The second most popular field of study is business, with the social sciences and humanities and arts tied for third place, as shown in the bar graph on the next page.

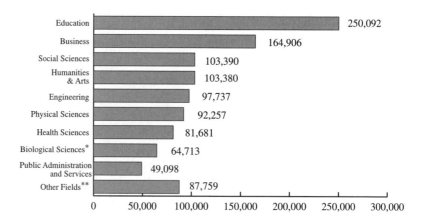

* Includes agriculture.
** Includes architecture, communications, home economics, library sciences, and religion.

Graduate Enrollment by Field, 1996.

Source: Council of Graduate Schools/GRE Survey of Graduate Enrollment.

In almost all the fields of study shown on the graph on page 10, enrollment increased until the mid-1990s and then flattened or fell. The exceptions to this downward trend are business, education, and health sciences. No doubt these areas have done better because degrees in these fields are closely tied to career advancement.

WHAT GRADUATE SCHOOL IS LIKE

As an undergraduate, you were probably one among many. You took courses in a wide range of subjects, sometimes along with hundreds of other students. You went to class, studied, and took exams. Perhaps you got to know one or two faculty members. After you had passed a certain number of courses, you earned your bachelor's degree.

In contrast, as a graduate student you will be among students who share your interests and enthusiasm. If you are enrolled full-time, the faculty members are more likely to get to know you. In many programs your courses will consist of small classes and seminars. You will be expected not merely to pass these courses, but also to do well. After a while, you will have to narrow your focus of interest in your field and choose a specialty. You will be expected to do independent work, and that requires a high level of self-discipline. However, if you're lucky, you are working with faculty members who are tops in your chosen field and with other intelligent people who share your interest in a subject. According to Melany Kahn, who earned an M.F.A. in film from New York University, one of the best things about graduate school was the camaraderie of her fellow students. They were "one of the greatest assets of going through a grad program....You will work with these people for a long time, in the working world as well as in school."

Earning a Master's Degree

It usually takes a full-time student one to three years to complete the requirements for a master's degree. You must take courses in certain areas. At some point, you choose an area of specialization within your subject area. If you are in the sciences, you may have less flexibility in choosing an area of specialization because you are required to do lab research or field work under the supervision of a faculty member. Thus, your choices are limited to the research areas of interest to the faculty members in your department. If you are in a professional program, you may do internships that introduce you to work in your field.

In some master's programs, you must take exams that demonstrate your mastery of the field when your course work is done. These may be oral, written, or both. In some programs, you must also write a master's thesis. Sometimes the thesis involves original research, but it may simply be a long paper on a specific topic.

Earning a Doctoral Degree

Candidates in an academic doctoral program usually pick up a master's degree along the way to the Ph.D. The Ph.D. is similar in some ways to the master's, but the bar is raised in all areas. Two or three years of course work are followed by comprehensive exams. Often called "orals," these are graded by a small committee of faculty members from your department. Needless to say, most graduate students dread these exams. Still, they provide an impetus for students to delve into the subject and work closely with professors. It's not uncommon for students to spend anywhere from a few months to a couple of years preparing for the comprehensive exams.

> Graduate school is not like college, only harder. It's more like having a challenging job that requires an enormous commitment of time and energy but doesn't pay very well, if at all.

Once you pass the qualifying exams, you are ready to move on to the dissertation stage. By this time you should have a pretty good idea of a "problem" in your discipline that you wish to tackle for your dissertation. Unlike a master's thesis, a Ph.D. dissertation involves original research and it is usually much longer. The research must be original and the result must make a contribution to the body of knowledge in your field.

In the humanities, most of the research is conducted in libraries, using books and journals. You want to make sure that your theme has not already been dealt with in the same way that you propose to approach it. In addition, you must prove that the sources used support your approach. In the social sciences your research may involve field work. In the sciences, the faculty member under whom you work has already done much of the preliminary research. As his or her apprentice, you help conduct experiments in the lab and research. You use this apprenticeship experience to write a dissertation on some aspect of the research in which you have taken part.

Researching and writing a dissertation usually takes years. To keep you on track and guide the research and writing, you choose a dissertation committee of three to five faculty members. During the dissertation period, you may come to know more about your area of specialization than anyone in your department, so the advice you get from your committee may be general rather than specific. Your adviser, the chair of the committee, has the principal responsibility for guiding you through the dissertation process. Ideally, the members of your committee get along with one another and if any disagreements arise, your adviser is skilled at advocacy, diplomacy, and negotiation.

A good adviser becomes the graduate student's mentor. He or she gives you the benefit of years of expertise, helps you deal with unfriendly criticism, and introduces you to people who may be useful professional contacts. Part of your graduate education is to begin to establish yourself in the field by attending conferences and networking and a good mentor helps you with this.

Still, for the most part, you will be on your own. You will need the self-discipline to do your work for several years without someone supplying you with daily instructions and interim assignments and deadlines. Basically, at this stage you will need to work and think independently. Still, intellectual excitement keeps many students going. As Dan Stollenwerk, who has advanced degrees in theology, put it, "The freedom to think and study is the best thing about the life of a graduate student."

For many Ph.D. candidates, that freedom is somewhat curtailed because they are also teaching or are research assistants who work for their professors in the classroom or the lab. However, teaching classes or doing research has two main benefits: it enables you to pay for graduate school and to gain practical experience. Still, students who work must find a balance between pursuing their own studies and fulfilling their work responsibilities.

So, you can see that preparing a dissertation is a long and difficult process. The situation is so unstructured that many people simply cannot see it through. Many graduate students falter at this stage and never complete their dissertations. They leave their programs as ABDs "all but dissertation," an acronym of no academic value. However, others are so energized by the opportunity to work on a problem of their own choosing that they have plenty of inner motivation to continue working on their dissertations.

Once you have drafted your dissertation, your committee reviews it and offers suggestions for revisions. You go back and revise the draft, producing a final version. You are now ready for the last step: defending your dissertation. You appear before your committee and respond orally to questions and comments about your research, thesis, arguments, and conclusions. Although the oral defense is another anxiety-producing hurdle for graduate students, failure is rare. After all, the same people who are questioning you now have been supervising your research and writing for the last few years. They want you to succeed.

GETTING INTO GRADUATE SCHOOL

Still interested in graduate school? Then the next question is: what's involved in finding and getting into a graduate program? A lot. So much, in fact, that you should start the process at least a year and a half to two years before you plan to enroll.

The first, and perhaps the most important part of the application process is a combination of introspection and research. You are going to have to assess yourself and assess what's out there to find a good match. You'll have to answer questions like, What are my professional goals? What are my interests and abilities? Which degree will help me achieve my goals? Am I qualified for graduate work? Did my undergraduate courses prepare me for higher education in this field? What must I do to improve my qualifications? Which programs are most likely to help me reach my goals? Which programs do I have a realistic chance of getting into? In Chapters 2 and 3, we will help you assess your strengths and weaknesses and gather information about specific programs.

Once you've done your research on graduate programs, on what basis should you evaluate them? You'll have to go beyond the annual university rankings and graduate school directories to find out what each graduate program is really like and whether it's a good match for you. How can you get solid information about the programs in which you are interested in order to make an informed judgment? How can you narrow your choices so you have no more than a half dozen or so to which you will apply? Chapter 4 discusses these issues and provides a checklist of factors you should consider when evaluating programs.

Once you've identified the programs to which you will apply, what standardized qualifying exams, if any, will you need to take? What should you do to prepare for the Graduate Record Examination (GRE) or one of the graduate admissions examinations used by the professional schools? Chapter 5 covers preparing for and taking the graduate admissions tests.

Then the application process begins. Unfortunately, applying to graduate school is not as standardized a process as applying to college. You will have to find out what each program requires and what the deadlines are. You may be sending some forms to a central graduate admissions office and other forms directly to the department or school to which you are applying. You may be writing a personal statement so that the admissions committee can evaluate whether you will be an asset to their program. You'll be asking professors or colleagues to write letters of recommendation. Preparing your applications carefully and keeping track of them is extremely important. In Chapters 6 and 7, we'll describe the process in more detail and give you suggestions on how to prepare applications and write essays that will gain you admission.

How are you going to pay for your graduate education? If you are planning to attend part-time while working, that may not be a problem. But for full-time students, financing a graduate education can be complicated and the competition for funding is considerable. You will have to figure out how much money you will need, find possible sources of aid, and apply for them. Chapter 8 covers financing your graduate education.

Once you have received offers of admission, you will have to make a decision. Which offer should you accept? Chapter 9 offers suggestions on how to find the inside scoop about a program so you will be able to make your final selection with confidence.

Finally, in Chapter 10, some of the graduate students we interviewed and surveyed will share more of their experiences and offer additional advice.

In the pages that follow, there are many suggestions for accomplishing all of the tasks involved in selecting and applying to graduate programs. Not all of the advice will be applicable to everyone. Still, this book will provide you with an overview of what you will need to know. And it will indicate what you will need to find out on your own to ensure that your graduate education does all that you hope it will do.

Assessing Yourself

Chapter 2

So far, we have considered graduate education in a broad sense. But, as you will see, you will have to attend to many details before embarking on a graduate career. You will have to find the right match between you and a graduate program and prepare yourself to submit the best possible application. In this chapter, we'll discuss the first thing you should do before you even start looking for programs—a self-assessment that will be the starting point of your evaluation of graduate education. An honest and thorough self-assessment will enable you to identify the degree you should pursue and reduce your program choices to a more manageable number.

TIMETABLE

Finding appropriate graduate programs, taking qualifying tests, and assembling all the parts of an application is a time-consuming process. Admissions and financial aid decisions are often made about six months before enrollment, so you should begin your preliminary self-assessment, research, and applications at least a year before that. That means starting the whole process a year and a half to two years before you wish to begin your graduate studies. Starting early will give you time to consider your goals, research your opportunities, decide on the programs to which you will apply, request information and applications, take qualifying exams, prepare your applications, and apply for financial assistance. A timeline that will help you pace the application process appears in Appendix 1.

QUESTIONS TO ASK YOURSELF

Before you expend a great deal of effort, a little soul-searching is in order. The first step in getting into graduate school involves assessing your goals, abilities, qualifications, temperament, and commitment.

This type of assessment can be difficult, especially for undergraduates, who have had less time and opportunity to get to know themselves in a variety of settings, both academic and nonacademic. People whose college days are several years behind them often find it easier to articulate their goals and evaluate their strengths and weaknesses. Nevertheless, whether you find it easy or hard, you should answer the following questions honestly.

What are my long-term goals? What would I like to be doing in five or ten years? Will a graduate degree help me achieve my long-term goals?

These are the three most important questions to answer before you search for graduate school. Once you have answered these questions, then you can start to look for a program that will help you achieve your goals. Students who get the most out of their graduate educations tend to be very focused. They know what they want, and they have chosen their degree program because they believe it will help them achieve their goals.

One student who knew exactly what she was after was Naaz Qureshi. After earning a B.A. in political science from the University of Texas at Austin, Qureshi worked for Chase Manhattan Bank as a small business banker, underwriting loans according to strict guidelines. After a while, she decided that she wanted a job that allowed her to be more creative. "I realized that the only way to transition into another position would be through an M.B.A.," says Qureshi. "This degree would give me the necessary business skills that I lacked, having a liberal arts degree." Qureshi is now a student at the Cox School of Business of Southern Methodist University in Dallas, Texas.

Another student saw graduate school as a way to pursue a long-held dream. While growing up, Cindy Liutkus used to read about human evolution and the Leakey family's excavations in Africa. She dreamed of someday working there. As an undergraduate majoring in philosophy and geology, Liutkus decided that graduate school would open the door to fulfilling her childhood dream. Because she wants to teach at the university level, she is now pursuing a Ph.D. in geology at

Rutgers University in New Jersey. Her first field trip? She studied ancient sediments at Olduvai Gorge in Tanzania.

Leslie Nelman saw a graduate degree as a way to shift gears into a "pre-retirement" job. After twenty-two years in the business world, eight of them at the executive level, she was looking for something that would allow her to work independently and combine her experience in investments, insurance, and law with her ability to speak German. When she found out there was a high demand for freelance translators with her background, she knew she had found a career that would suit her needs perfectly. Nelman is now enrolled at the Monterey Institute of International Studies in California where she is earning a Master of Arts in translation and interpretation.

Melany Kahn's realization that she wanted to go back to school came to her almost out of the blue: "I was sitting in a meditation course, thinking when you aren't supposed to be thinking, about what I had liked about my previous job. I had been in charge of PR at a nonprofit organization, and I had made two films there. My favorite part had been editing them. In order to be able to do more of that kind of work, it occurred to me to apply to film school." Today, Melanie has an M.F.A. in film from New York University, and she is teaching there.

Of course, there are people—and you may be one of them—who don't know exactly what they want to accomplish professionally. Instead, they have a general idea. For example, David Watkins, a computer science major, wasn't sure whether he wanted to work in industry or become a college professor. Still, he figured that either way he would benefit from having a master's degree. After a year in the master's program in computer science at Virginia Tech, Watkins has decided to look for a job in industry after he finishes his degree. So for Watkins and many other students, the experience they gain in graduate school serves to clarify their goals.

Do I enjoy this field of study so much that I can picture myself spending most of my time on it for years to come?

In graduate school, you will be spending a lot of time on a particular subject in preparation for related work in that subject. Can you imagine

> Gladys Fleckles, director of graduate studies at California State University at Fullerton, sums up the degree-choosing process this way: "I believe that at one level, you can pursue a degree for the love of learning. But for an advanced degree, you also have to be practical. You have to consider what you want to be when you 'grow up.' Choosing a degree is almost a career counseling exercise."

devoting a good part of your life to that field? As Maria Vesperi, Associate Professor of Anthropology at New College, the honors college of Florida's state university system, puts it, "If you don't have a sustained interest in your subject now, how interested will you be when you are doing it eight hours a day? Do something that you love to do." Adds Stephanie Muntone, who earned an M.A. in history with a certificate in archival management from New York University, "Go with whatever interests you the most. The implication of getting a graduate degree is that you are going to be associated with this field for a large part of your life—so choose something you are genuinely interested in. If you are interested in something, you can find a way to make it pay."

Should I go to graduate school straight from college or work for a few years first?

There are arguments on both sides of this question. If you are going straight through, adjusting to graduate school may be easier because you are still in the habit of doing a lot of reading, synthesizing, writing papers, and taking exams. You also won't have time to forget a lot of what you've learned, something that's especially important for students in the sciences: "...Mathematics is not like riding a bicycle. You do forget how," says Neill Kipp, a Ph.D. candidate in computer science at Virginia Tech. Another advantage you have is that you are unlikely to have many other claims on your time and resources. According to Kimani Toussaint, an engineering student at Boston University, graduate school is "definitely something that you should do when you have the least at stake. In my case, I don't have a family and don't really have any expenses."

However, there is a lot to be said for working for a few years. If you are an older student, you are—surprise!—more mature. You probably have a much clearer idea of what you want to do now than you did when you were twenty. If you do go back to school, you know why you are there and what you want to get out of the experience. This means that you are motivated and focused. You may have more trouble adjusting to graduate school than a younger student does, but your life experience will probably compensate for rusty skills. Even though many older

Although many older students express a wish that they had done their graduate work when they were in their twenties and had fewer commitments, when queried, they usually acknowledge that they were not ready for graduate school when they were younger.

students express a wish that they had done their graduate work when they were in their twenties and had fewer commitments, when queried they usually acknowledge that they were not ready for grad school when they were younger.

The short answer to this question is: no matter what your age, if you don't have a clear idea of your goals, you should probably wait. Many students go on to graduate school straight from college because they have no other plans. They've been in school all their lives and they simply can't visualize themselves doing anything else. That's not a good reason to be there.

Do I have an aptitude for the type of work I will be doing in graduate school?

Graduate work, no matter what the field, involves a great deal of reading, synthesizing, and writing. And depending on your field of interest, it may involve lab work, hands-on projects, field work, or library research. Can you do this type of work? If so, will you enjoy it?

If you have been working for a few years, you may be out of the habit of doing many of these things. Perhaps the longest piece of writing you've done lately is an interoffice memo, and your most challenging reading is the newspaper. Think back to your undergraduate days. That will give you a better basis on which to evaluate whether you can do the type of work that graduate school requires.

Do I have the academic and professional qualifications that will enable me to pursue this degree? If not, what do I have to do to make up for my lack of qualifications?

Although theoretically you may not need a bachelor's degree in order to pursue a particular graduate degree, in practice a bachelor's degree is a minimum requirement for most programs. For some professional degrees, such as a master of library science, a law degree, or an M.B.A., your undergraduate major is not a critical factor in the admissions decision. But for other degrees, your undergraduate courses will be important. Because there is no single academic standard, you must check the academic prerequisites of the programs in which you are interested. For example, if you are interested in pursuing a doctoral degree in experimental psychology, how many courses in psychology will you be expected to have taken as an undergraduate, and at what level? Typically, if you were a psychology major in college, you will be adequately prepared for graduate work in psychology.

Suppose, however, that you hope to use the graduate degree to switch to a new field in which you have little or no academic background. Under these circumstances, what will you need to do to improve your qualifications?

Perhaps one or two college-level courses, a certificate program, or a research assistantship will be enough to convince an admissions committee that you are committed to your new field. For example, one student who had majored in sociology wanted to switch to anthropology as a graduate student, but she had taken only two anthropology courses in college. The first time she applied to graduate programs in anthropology, she was turned down everywhere. She then spent a year assisting a professor at an archaeological dig before reapplying. With this experience added to her qualifications, this time she was accepted.

Another student made an even bigger switch—from African American studies to electrical engineering—and he found a program that would help him do it. As a senior at the University of Pennsylvania, Kimani Toussaint became interested in photonics and decided to pursue advanced studies and a career in science and engineering. In the course of researching programs in the Peterson's guides to graduate education, Toussaint found the Late Entry Accelerated Program (LEAP) at Boston University. This program is designed to give people with backgrounds in other fields a crash course in a field of engineering. Incoming graduate students take some undergraduate courses and then phase into graduate work. "I remember thinking that the LEAP program is analogous to the post-bac programs that many aspiring medical students enroll in," says Toussaint. Toussaint earned an M.S. and is currently pursuing a doctoral degree in electrical engineering at Boston University.

Another area in which people are sometimes weak academically is their undergraduate grade point average. However, if you think that your other strengths eclipse your GPA and you can demonstrate that

> **Although theoretically you may not need a bachelor's degree in order to pursue a particular graduate degree, in practice, a bachelor's degree is a minimum requirement for most programs.**

you've changed your ways and are now a hard-working individual, you should not let a weak GPA stop you. You may be able to compensate for a poor undergraduate GPA in other areas of your application.

In addition to your academic background, your professional background can be an important factor in determining whether you are admitted to a graduate program. This is especially true of M.B.A. and social work programs, which generally look for candidates who have several years of work experience beyond the baccalaureate degree. It is also true of many of the professional graduate degree programs, which may consider related work experience as a demonstration of sustained interest in the field. For example, Joyce May worked for her town's public library system for several years before applying to a master's program in library and information science at the University of Rhode Island. Her work background was a positive factor on her application.

In summary, if you feel your academic or professional qualifications fall short of what's needed for graduate school, you should not necessarily let that stop you. Like the students described above, you can improve your qualifications through additional study, research, or work.

Do I have the motivation, self-discipline, self-confidence, interpersonal skills, and persistence required to earn a graduate degree?

Whether or not you succeed in graduate school will depend on your intellectual skills and abilities, but you also will need will-power and positive personal characteristics. Graduate study is much more independent than undergraduate study. Do you have the motivation and self-discipline to work on your own toward your goals? Do you have the self-confidence to persist in your studies even when things are not going well or your professors are not giving you much feedback?

Heather Helms-Erikson recalls her first semester as a master's candidate in marriage and family therapy at the University of Maryland. "I was used to constant feedback from teachers," says Helms-Erikson, who had attended a very small liberal arts college in Pennsylvania. "But there was very little feedback until the one exam and one paper were graded at the end of the term. It made me very insecure, and I thought I had made a horrible mistake." Once Helms-Erikson got some positive feedback from her professors, her confidence in her own abilities was restored and she finished her course work. "You need the self-discipline to work independently," she says. Jenn Wagaman, who is studying for a master's degree in public communications at the University of Alaska at Fairbanks, loves the independence of graduate school. "Everything you choose is your own, including how much you study and how much time you invest. The best part is the feeling that my work is directly related to my future."

But some people feel overwhelmed by the demands of graduate school. When she was in her twenties and a Ph.D. candidate in linguistics at Ohio State, Jean Godby says she was "gripped by a fear of failure. It turned me into a workaholic, which was psychologically destructive and not even professionally fruitful. I dropped out when I was ABD." After many years, some of which she spent as a research scientist in linguistics, Jean resumed her candidacy. She had acquired the self-confidence she needed to complete the degree. "All of this went very smoothly because it turned out I was ahead of them in my area of expertise," comments Godby.

Your ability to get along with others may also be critical to your success in graduate school. One purpose of graduate education is to make you a colleague, not only of your fellow students, but of your professors as well. To accomplish this is both an intellectual and an interpersonal challenge. In addition, some graduate programs promote teamwork among students. In the sciences and engineering, you may be working in research labs and on projects as a member of a team. In business school, you may often work on assignments and presentations as a member of a group.

A professor of anthropology who has seen many graduate students succeed and fail over the years, Jay Sokolovsky of the University of South Florida thinks that successful graduate students have two important qualities: the ability to synthesize a huge amount of material in a short time and intellectual persistence. Of these two qualities, he says, lack of persistence is the number one reason that students drop out: "It often comes down to, can you slog through and finish the writing?"

Am I willing to commit the time, effort, and personal and financial resources that pursuing a graduate degree requires?

A full-time master's candidate may spend two years earning a degree; a part-time student may take twice as long or longer. Doctoral candidates take from five to ten years to complete their degrees. And whether you are a full- or part-time student, you must commit most of your free time to your studies in order to keep up. As Felecia Bartow, who is studying for her Master of Social Work at Washington University in St. Louis, Missouri, commented: "In graduate school, there is always something that you could or should be doing, and it is harder to justify spending time on nonacademic activities."

Because of the time and effort demanded in graduate school, most other aspects of your life are going to take a back seat. If you have a family, your spouse and children may see little of you. "Life as a graduate student, wife, and mother of two preschool children was torture," says Renee Lantz, a doctoral candidate in fire protection engineering at Worcester Polytechnic Institute in Massachusetts. "I depended heavily on my husband, parents, in-laws, and neighbors to get by. The network of personal and family support made it physically possible for me to successfully complete the master's." According to Bartow, graduate school placed "extraordinary demands on...personal relationships. I am married and my husband agreed to leave his job and relocate to a different state so that I could pursue my graduate education....Thankfully, he recently finished an advanced degree in psychology and is extremely understanding about the time constraints I face."

Students attending part-time may also have difficulty balancing school with both family and work. "The most difficult adjustment I faced was balancing a full-time job; my home life, including a teenager with a very busy sports schedule; and school deadlines," says Andrea Edwards Myers, a master's candidate in public communications at the College of St. Rose in Albany, New York. Laurie Noe, an Ed.D.

> "In graduate school, there is always something that you could or should be doing, and it is harder to justify spending time on nonacademic activities."

candidate in a distance learning program at Nova Southeastern University, echoed Myers's words: "Juggling my time between personal, professional, and academic commitments is the most difficult thing about grad school."

These students, and many others, did find a way to balance school with their personal and professional commitments. For many of them, this balancing act was one of the hardest things about graduate school and having a supportive family was crucial to their success. Says Brenda Bennett, who received a Master of Special Education degree from Cambridge College in Massachusetts, "I didn't cook dinner for a year; my husband did. What a great guy!"

Another aspect of graduate education that can cause problems, especially for full-time students, is finances. Students lucky enough to receive financial aid that covers tuition and provides a stipend usually have enough to live on—but just barely. For many students, that is enough. According to Dan Stollenwerk, who earned several degrees in theology, "There is no life like a student's. You always have money even though you are always poor. You can always afford a movie and a beer; and even though you have no insurance, you have nothing to insure."

For students returning to school full-time after a period of working, the lower standard of living may come as a shock. "I had money and a good job and I gave that up. I don't have the resources now even to take a break for recreation," says Helms-Erikson. And for those who have been living this way for years, the lower standard of living can become a sore point. "I'm almost 30 now," says Kimberly Tremblay, a postdoctoral candidate in developmental biology at Harvard, "and I have no car, and for the first time since I was a freshman in college I needed to get a roommate to help pay the rent. It's tough now, but it's worth it for the future."

GETTING CAREER COUNSELING

If you have trouble doing this self-assessment on your own or want a more objective look at your capabilities, you can find a counselor or consultant to help you. If you are still in school, you can ask a counselor at your college's career development or placement office to help you assess your strengths and weaknesses, discover your aptitudes, and match them with potential careers, and by extension, graduate degrees. Or, you can hire an independent counselor to advise you. To find this type of help, you can contact the National Board for Certified Counselors at 800-398-5389 or www.nbcc.org and they will send you a list of certified counselors in your area.

One advantage of using professional career counselors is that they will be objective about your skills, aptitudes, and potential. This can be especially helpful if you are worried about being unduly influenced by others, such as parents or close friends, who have their own ideas about what you should do. Career counselors can also help you avoid two common pitfalls: overestimating yourself and underestimating yourself. You want to have a pretty good idea of who you are and what you want professionally before you spend much time researching graduate programs, whether you come to this self-knowledge on your own or with professional help.

Career counselors can also help you avoid two common pitfalls: overestimating yourself and underestimating yourself.

Locating Information

Chapter 3

Now that you have taken the time and trouble to answer the self-assessment questions in Chapter 2, your search for information about graduate school will be a little easier. For one thing, you will have articulated your long-term goals and narrowed your areas of interest. You may have already decided which degree is best for you: a master's, a Ph.D., or a professional certificate. If your field of interest is very narrow, your choices may be limited and your search very easy. For example, Megan McAfee was looking for a master's program in costume technology, a field in which there are only a few programs, so her research did not take long. On the other hand, Kimberly Tremblay's focus on biology, a field with many subspecialties and programs, required considerably more investigation.

Other factors may make your search for information straightforward and relatively simple. If you have established roots in an area and don't wish to move, you will be looking for programs within commuting distance or distance learning programs. If you are working full-time, you will need to find a local or distance learning program that offers a part-time degree program. If you don't expect to receive financial aid and money is tight, you may consider only public institutions. Whatever your interests and situation, there are many sources of information that will provide general advice about graduate school as well as help you identify programs that may meet your needs. Some of the most helpful resources are discussed here and additional resources are listed in Appendix 2.

THE INTERNET

The Internet is an excellent place to begin your search for information about graduate education. The amount of information can be overwhelming, but here are some suggestions for getting started on your search. The Web sites discussed below provide general information on graduate school and help with finding programs (sources of information about financial aid will be discussed in Chapter 8). Remember that Internet addresses sometimes change, so if you are having trouble finding a particular site, search for it using the name of the organization that maintains it.

General Information Web Sites

There are several Web sites that offer general information, news, and advice of interest to prospective graduate students. These sites are useful if you are still gathering background information about graduate education. Many of them provide links to more specific resources on the Internet.

Creative Learning Services, Inc. maintains a very useful gateway Web site called Resources for Graduate Students (http://www. problemfinder.com). This site has links to dozens of sites of interest to graduate students, including sites on financial aid and distance learning. You can explore career and occupational outlooks and connect to online research resources at major universities, arranged by field of study. In addition, you can subscribe to the site's informational newsletter to stay abreast of issues and events in the world of graduate education.

The Council of Graduate Schools hosts a site that provides links to recent articles about graduate education (http://www.cgsnet.org). There is a lot of information on the state of graduate education today, including political issues that affect graduate students, such as changes to the tax code and government financial aid. In addition, the section "Of Interest to Students" provides lots of general information about graduate education as well as information of particular interest to women, members of minority groups, and international students.

If you are interested in sampling some graduate theses or learning more about the thesis-writing process, visit the Web site of the Association for Support of Graduate Students (http://www.asgs.org).

This organization maintains a site that provides a forum for academic reading and discussion. It also has a more informal forum, called Doc-Talk, in which students from all over the world post messages about doing a thesis.

Online Graduate Program Directories

Many of the searchable databases and directories of schools of higher education on the Internet are designed primarily for high school students and do not use the type of focused search criteria that are important for prospective graduate students. However, there are a few sites that have search capabilities that are more suitable for graduate students.

One of the most comprehensive of these is on the Peterson's Web site (http://www.petersons.com). Peterson's, an education-information provider and publisher of college directories and other education-related materials (including this book), provides online access to current information distilled from its six-volume directory of graduate programs. The search capabilities are sophisticated: you can search their database by field of study, institution, a faculty member's name, or key word, phrase, or sentence. If you enter a field of study, information about the programs that offer degrees in this field is provided. If a particular program interests you, you can often submit an online request for more information and access its Web site through a hyperlink. The searchable databases include general graduate programs, business schools, law schools, medical schools, nursing programs, visual and performance arts programs, distance learning programs, executive education programs, and international student graduate programs.

Another searchable directory of graduate programs, produced by Educational Directories Unlimited, is available at http://www. gradschools. com. You can use this advertiser-supported directory as a means of identifying programs that meet your needs, although its search capabilities are not as sophisticated as Peterson's. You select your field of interest, such as communications, and then select the subfield in which you are interested, such as journalism. Once you run the search, you get a list of schools that offer degrees in that field. If the search results in too many hits, you narrow it further by region or state. Thus, to get all the schools offering a degree in journalism, you need to cycle through each region of the country, in turn. The information you finally get may be minimal: the school's or program's name and a link to its Web site. However, it is a good starting point for identifying schools that you should investigate further, especially if location is an important factor to you.

For international students who need to improve their English, Study in the U.S.A., Inc., maintains a site with a list of graduate schools that have an intensive English program (http://www.studyusa.com). The directory is not exhaustive, and it does not list professional schools. However, brief program descriptions are available in several languages and you can request further information online. The site also offers advice on taking qualifying tests, including the Test of English as a Foreign Language (TOEFL), obtaining a visa, and applying for admission.

Online Professional Directories and Information

Business School

In addition to searching the business school database on the Peterson's Web site, students interested in M.B.A. programs can visit the GMAT site (http://www.gmat.org). Although the best part of this site is its information about the GMAT, it also offers general information about the M.B.A. degree as well as a searchable database of business schools and advice about the application process.

Law School

For law school, the Internet Legal Resource Guide is the place to start (http://www.ilrg.com). This comprehensive site offers links to thousands of law-related Web sites. Of particular interest to prospective law students are the law school rankings, which explains the methodologies used to rank schools; a cost-benefit analysis comparing postgraduation salaries adjusted for regional differences in cost of living; and advice for prelaw students.

For students in the first stages of locating law schools, Boston College's Online Law School Locator is another excellent resource (http://www.bc.edu:80/bc_org/svp/carct/matrix.html). On a matrix, you select the intersection of your grade point average and Law School Admissions Test (LSAT) score, and you are given a list of law schools whose first year students have GPAs and scores similar to yours. This service enables you to identify a range of schools—from long shots to safety schools—so that you can apply to a good mix.

Medical School

Premed students, besides searching the Peterson's medical school database discussed above, can get the unofficial inside scoop on medical schools from current and recently graduated medical students at the Interactive Medical Student Lounge (http://www.geocities.com/Heartland/1756/lounge.html). Although you have to approach the information here somewhat cautiously, you can still learn a lot about medical school. In addition, there are lists of current students who are willing to answer premed students' questions about their medical schools.

University Web Sites

By now, almost every program and school in the nation has a Web site. The Web sites may be comprehensive and sophisticated, with everything from online applications and catalogs to e-mail links to faculty members, or they simply may be descriptive and provide you with street addresses to which you can write for further information. There is no standard for content or quality on the Web, so just keep in mind that each university and program is using its site as a marketing tool as well as a communications tool. Nevertheless, a program's Web site is an excellent entry point for gathering information about degrees, courses, faculty, and research areas.

Gail Ashley, professor of geological sciences at Rutgers University in New Jersey, says that her program's Web site has changed the way she interacts with prospective students. In the past, she responded to inquiries by writing a letter, which was time consuming. Now, she often gets e-mail inquiries from students gathering information on the Web, and a correspondence often ensues. "Gradually we find out if we might be suitable for one another," Ashley says. "E-mail is an easy and efficient way to do this."

PRINT MEDIA

Much of the information you can gather on the Internet is also available in print form. Your college's career counseling center or library, local public library, or bookstore will have many books you can tap into while investigating graduate school.

Peterson's Directories

Prospective graduate students will find much of the information they need to research and compare graduate schools in directories of graduate programs. These list universities and colleges along with the degrees they offer. They briefly describe the institution's facilities, number of faculty members and students, tuition, fees, and similar information and give the address, phone number, and Internet address of the institution. One of the serendipitous by-products of using a large print directory is that while browsing you may encounter interesting programs that you had not realized existed, as Kimani Toussaint did when he found Boston University's LEAP program, which provided a means for him to make the transition from African-American studies to engineering.

The six-volume Peterson's Guide to Graduate and Professional Programs, updated annually, is the most comprehensive and well-known of the directories, listing virtually every program at 1,700 institutions of higher learning. You can find the guide at most libraries or you can buy one or more volumes in a bookstore or on the Peterson's Web site. The six volumes include (1) an overview of graduate education; (2) humanities, arts, and social sciences; (3) biological sciences; (4) physical sciences, math, agricultural sciences, environment, and natural resources; (5) engineering and applied sciences; and (6) business, education, health, information studies, law, and social work. Keep in mind when using the Peterson's guides that the basic survey information is published in a paragraph, and that schools can choose to include a fuller description. Don't overlook the programs that lack a long description; it just means their administrators have not elected to include an additional statement. In addition, Peterson's publishes smaller one-volume guides focused on narrower areas of study as part of its Quick Focus Grad Series.

In addition to general directories, there are directories of the major professional degree programs. *Peterson's M.B.A. Programs 2000* covers more than 2,500 business programs throughout the world. The *Official Guide to U.S. Law Schools*, published by the Law School Admissions Council, devotes two pages each to law schools accredited by the American Bar Association. The Association of American Medical Colleges publishes *Medical School Admissions Requirements*, which contains up-to-date profiles on medical schools as well as advice on applying.

ADVISERS, PROFESSORS, STUDENTS AND COLLEAGUES

One of the best ways to find out about graduate programs is to talk to people who are in a position to know—advisers, professors, students, and alumni. If you are still in college, you have easy access to your own academic adviser, professors in the field in which you are interested, advisers in your college's career development or placement office, and alumni who may have employment experience in your field.

The career development office is an excellent place to do research and to talk to people with counseling experience. You may find many of the books and directories discussed above, in addition to reference material on employment. In addition, advisers can help you narrow your interests with personal counseling or by directing you to computerized self-assessment programs. Many offices can also put you in touch with alumni in your field of interest.

Your academic adviser and professors are a good source of information about graduate school. Talk with professors in the areas in which you are interested, and get their recommendations about graduate programs. "Professors like to talk about their fields," says Gladys Fleckles, director of graduate studies at California State University in Fullerton. "Ask where the top researchers are. Ask what they are doing." Professors usually know what type of work is being done at the major programs in their fields. If they have sent other students on to graduate schools in the past, find out what happened to those individuals.

Felecia Bartow, who is earning an M.S.W. at Washington University in St. Louis, also thinks it is important to talk to graduate students.

> If you cannot find a book about the professional degree in which you are interested, contact the professional association for information. For example, Heather Helms-Erikson wrote to the American Association for Marriage and Family Therapy for information about master's programs. They sent her a list of accredited programs in marriage and family therapy, which she used to narrow her choices.

"I would locate someone who has graduated from or is currently enrolled in the programs that interest you the most. I think you can get a better perspective about a school and its program from someone who has experienced it firsthand."

If you are attending a large university with graduate programs, talk to graduate students to find out what their programs are really like. Sit in on graduate courses and talk to faculty members involved in graduate education to get their recommendations. If there are informational graduate studies workshops given on campus or nearby, attend one.

If you've been out of school for a while, it may be more difficult for you to find people who can give you good information and advice. However, there are several things you can do to locate advisers, faculty members, students, and alumni who may be of help to you. You can contact your alma mater's career development office; most allow alumni to use their resources. You can also contact your former professors and ask to talk to them about graduate education. They may be able to refer you to faculty members in your field of interest at other schools. Or, you can see whether your state permits residents who are not students to use the career development office at a public institution of higher learning.

You can also use your professional contacts, the graduate program directories, or the Internet to find people in your field of interest. You will find that once you explain what you are trying to do, most people—even strangers—will be happy to tell you about themselves and give you advice!

DELVING DEEPER

One way to find out more about programs is to investigate the faculty members and research that they are doing. In fact, some students start their winnowing process by first identifying the area of research in which they are interested, and then doing a search of the literature to find people publishing in this area. To facilitate his search for a graduate program in computer science, David Watkins explains, "I first decided what I was interested in learning and then looked for schools that were performing a lot of research in that area."

"If you know specifically what area of research interests you, call the department at a school you are interested in, and ask to speak to faculty members in that area," advises Kimberly Tremblay, who is doing postdoctoral study in developmental biology at Harvard. Or, you can do as Professor Gail Ashley suggests: contact faculty members by e-mail and correspond with them to find out if your interests match theirs.

GETTING CATALOGS AND APPLICATIONS

Interviews, directories, and online databases are great to get you started, but once you've identified some programs of interest, you need to get further information from the schools themselves. You can send for catalogs and brochures by e-mail, through the program's Web site, by phone, or the old-fashioned way—by writing a letter or postcard. Don't bother asking professors for these; contact the program office or the graduate school admissions office to ask for catalogs and application forms. When you see how long it takes for you to get some of this material in the mail, you will begin to understand why it is important to start the application process a year and a half to two years before enrollment!

"If you know specifically what area of research interests you, call the department at a school you are interested in, and ask to speak to faculty members in that area."

Selecting Programs

In Chapter 3, you learned of various ways to gather information about graduate programs. If you have done your research, you are now surrounded by growing stacks of brochures, catalogs, Web page print-outs, application packets, and so on. Evaluating this barrage of information and selecting the programs to which you will apply are two of the more important tasks you face during the application process. If you approach these tasks wisely, you can greatly increase the likelihood of being accepted by a program that fits your needs.

How many programs should you be looking for? That depends on your personal situation. For example, Tom Fuchs had roots in San Diego and preferred not to move in order to get a graduate degree. When he researched psychology programs within commuting distance, he found that only three institutions offered what he needed. Of those three, only one, the California School of Professional Psychology, had a program with the strong practical, clinical focus that appealed to him. So he applied only to that one program, and he got in.

That approach, however, has obvious risks. If your one application is rejected, you are back where you started—with no place to go and nothing to show for your effort. Needless to say, the more programs to which you apply, the more likely it is that you will be accepted somewhere. David Faust, Professor of Psychology at the University of Rhode Island, explains why. According to Faust, admissions committees usually agree on the best and worst candidates, but they often disagree on those whose qualifications put them in the middle of the range.

One admissions committee might grant more weight to your undergraduate grade point average than to your performance at an interview, for example. Another might pay more attention to your letters of recommendation. So if you apply to many programs, you improve your chances of meeting the approval of at least one admissions committee. Therefore, if location is not an important factor or you live in an area with many universities, you should be thinking about applying to at least half a dozen programs. Applying to many programs will optimize your chances of getting financial assistance, too.

If possible, those half dozen or more should represent a range of admission difficulty. Just as you may have done when applying to college, have at least one or two "safety" schools, several in the middle range, and one or two "reach" schools. Don't immediately dismiss schools you think you can't get into, because you can never be sure just what they are looking for in a given year—it might be someone like you.

When reviewing the materials sent to you by each program, remember that a great deal of it is marketing material. Look for substance, not glitz. Read critically. Always keep this question foremost in your mind: Does this program meet my needs? If the program's brochure is well done, it should answer most of your questions. But if you still need more information, don't hesitate to contact the department by phone or e-mail to ask questions or visit the campus and speak with people face to face. Any personal contacts you have with a program may help you later on if you decide to apply.

One of the first things you'll see in the brochures of many programs is a mission statement in which the program's goals, strategies, and philosophy are set forth. Evaluate the way each program presents itself, and eliminate those that you find unappealing. As Cathy Chappell, an Ed.D. candidate in educational foundations at the University of Cincinnati, explains, "If [the mission statement] makes you uncomfortable, don't apply there. It won't serve you well to go somewhere that is not right for you and your research."

If location is not an important factor or if you live in an area with many universities, you should be thinking about applying to at least half a dozen programs. Applying to many programs will optimize your chances of getting financial assistance, too.

FACTORS TO CONSIDER

What should you look for when you are selecting the programs to which you will apply? There are many factors you should consider, including the quality of the faculty members, opportunities for research or field work, the currency of the program, degree requirements, size and diversity of the student body, time, location, the university environment, accreditation, and so on. The importance you attach to each of these factors will depend on your personal needs and preferences. If you can determine what's really important to you, you will find the selection process a little easier. "Decide in advance on the two or three most important elements that you require from any program," advises Felecia Bartow, an M.S.W. candidate at Washington University in St. Louis. "Those elements could include cost, available classes, internship opportunities, faculty research interests, size and/or diversity of the student body, etc. For me, it was much easier to narrow down my choices when I stuck to the criteria that I had determined in advance."

The Faculty

The faculty are the people on whom a program's quality ultimately depends. They will influence your day-to-day life as a student, not to mention your future. So one of the most important things to look at when evaluating programs is the faculty.

If you have already narrowed your area of interest, look at the professors whose interests match yours. Where did they study? What have they published? How current is their work? Is their work well funded? What are their reputations? Remember that in some disciplines, such as the hard sciences, it can be more important to have worked under an individual with an outstanding reputation than at a university with a prestigious name.

In addition to considering the faculty's reputation in the field, you will have to consider whether the mentoring prospects are good, especially if your degree requires independent research and a thesis. Heather Helms-Erikson, a Ph.D. candidate in the Department of Human Development and Family Studies at the College of Health and Human Development of Pennsylvania State University, points out, "Even at a top institution, you won't get a great education unless you have a good mentor. It's hard to get your work done if you've got a famous adviser who is always traveling." How do faculty members treat their students? Do they work closely with students, nurturing their interests and involving them in their work? Or, as Neill Kipp, a Ph.D. candidate in computer science at Virginia Tech, so trenchantly puts it, do students feel that the faculty "steal all their glory while they slave away in the lab"?

If you are interested in professional programs, consider the faculty members' professional backgrounds as well as their academic backgrounds. Where have they studied? What positions have they held? In general, it is a plus if the faculty represents a balance between creative academicians and successful practitioners.

If the program looks interesting, get in touch with a couple of faculty members to discuss it. "You can tell a lot by whether the faculty members are willing to take the time to talk to a prospective student," says Jeanne Reesman, Interim Dean of Graduate Studies and Professor of English at the University of Texas at San Antonio. "If they are not willing to take the time, then don't go." Talking to current students will also help you get a better perspective on what a program is really like.

The Program's Reputation

How a program is viewed by outside experts or professors at other institutions tells you a great deal about its reputation. But don't confuse a program's professional reputation with its general prestige, which generally derives from the prestige of its institution.

You can get a sense of a program's reputation by examining the faculty's background. Does its faculty publish in the important journals? Are they appointed to professional governing boards or to governmental commissions? Do they garner significant internal and external financial support? For professional programs, you can check whether graduates go on to positions of importance in your field. You can also ask your undergraduate professors and professional colleagues for their opinions.

Another popular way to evaluate a program's reputation is to consult published national ratings, which are usually compiled by surveying scholars. The most recent large-scale survey was based on 16,000 faculty raters' opinions of 3,600 programs in forty-one disciplines and was conducted by the National Research Council. In 1995, the council published the results in *Research-Doctorate Programs in the United States*, otherwise known as the "Blue Book." In addition, annual ratings of graduate programs are published by *U.S. News & World Report* and *Business Week*, among other publications.

What exactly do these program ratings tell you? They tell you a lot about the *perception* of various programs, which may or may not have a close connection to the actual quality of the education provided. In most cases, programs that have academic stars or that are located on prestigious campuses are the ones that get the highest ratings. Thus, the ratings don't always correlate with other, perhaps more objective measures of achievement, such as the number of citations of professors' work by other scholars. So, if you do consult ratings, look at more than one set of them and remember that they reflect the prestige of the program, not necessarily its educational quality. Also keep in mind that the prestige of a program will mean little to you if the program is not a good match for you.

Program Versus University Reputation

It's important to separate the reputation of a program from the reputation of the university to which it belongs. Granted, in many cases, both program and university will have similar reputations. But in some cases, you may find a below average program at an excellent university or an above average program at a university with a lesser reputation. Again, you see why it's crucial that you do your homework on each program.

National Versus Regional Reputation

Many programs have excellent reputations in their regions but are not as well known nationally. Whether a program's reputation is regional or national may be a factor for you. If you are hoping to do research or teach at the university level or be recruited by top employers from around the nation, you should be looking at programs with national reputations.

Keep in mind that you can get an excellent education at an institution whose draw and reputation are primarily regional. Remember, however, that employment opportunities, both in academia and elsewhere, are likely to be regional as well. Says Naaz Qureshi, an M.B.A. candidate at Cox School of Business of Southern Methodist University in Dallas, "It is imperative to ask yourself if you wouldn't mind either staying there after graduation or working very hard to find a job elsewhere."

Accreditation

Colleges and universities in the United States, as well as individual departments and programs, are evaluated by nongovernmental regional and specialized agencies concerned with monitoring the quality of

It's important that you thoroughly understand the significance of accreditation in your field since it may affect your professional future as well as the quality of your education.

education. The agencies look at the school, program, or department's mission and how well it fulfills it, its financial and other resources, the quality of its academic offerings, and the level of services it provides. Those that pass muster are awarded accreditation by the evaluating agency. Even when the evaluating agency accredits a department or university, it may recommend that certain improvements be made. In addition, each department and school is reviewed every few years to ensure it continues to meet the established standards. If it does not, it may be put on probation or lose its accreditation altogether. Keep in mind that it is possible for a university to be accredited on an institutional level while one of its programs is not.

Accreditation is a complicated matter. In general, accreditation by a regional accrediting agency means that the institution or program has been around long enough to be well established and that the degree you earn will be generally accepted. In some disciplines, specialized as well as regional accreditation plays a role. In certain professional fields, such as medicine, it is necessary to have graduated from a program that is accredited in order to qualify for a license to practice. In some disciplines, the federal government also makes a degree from an accredited program a hiring requirement. But in other fields, accreditation is not as essential and you can find good programs that are not accredited. It's important that you thoroughly understand the significance of accreditation in your field since it may affect your professional future as well as the quality of your education.

To one master's candidate in library and information sciences, accreditation history was a prime consideration when she selected programs. She comments, "Grad students should aim to receive a degree which will be of value to them throughout their lives. The choice of institution will either open or close doors in the future."

To find out the accreditation status of the programs and institutions in which you are interested, you can ask them to provide information on their accreditation status in writing. Or, you may prefer to contact the accrediting agencies directly. The regional accrediting agencies are listed in Appendix 2; for specialized agencies, consult *Peterson's Guide to Professional and Graduate Programs, Volume 1.*

Academic Issues

Look at the catalog and determine whether the course offerings and curriculum are close to what you are seeking. How often are courses given? Is the curriculum challenging? Is it up to date? Does it emphasize what interests you? Does one school of thought or approach to research dominate? Will you have the option of working in other departments or with nearby institutions? Are there ample opportunities for field work or research? Are the program and school accredited?

In addition, be sure to read this material carefully to determine what requirements for the degree you will need to fulfill. Is there any flexibility in the requirements? If you have something in mind other than what the program usually requires, make sure they are open to new ideas before you apply. For example, Jim Lipuma, a Ph.D. candidate in environmental science at New Jersey Institute of Technology, was looking for a program that would allow him to do a dissertation on an environmental education policy research topic, a particularly multidisciplinary area of research. "Such versatility is difficult to find," says Lipuma. "I found few [programs] that might allow or could support such a flexible multidisciplinary dissertation."

Your Own Qualifications

Do you have the minimum academic and/or professional qualifications required of applicants to the program? Programs or universities may set minimum standards for grade point average, grade point average in your major subject, and/or graduate admissions test scores. In addition, there may be undergraduate course requirements that you must fulfill. If your past academic record is below the standard set by a program, you will have to find out whether they will consider making an exception for you if your application is otherwise strong or if you compensate for poor or lacking past performance by taking college- or graduate-level courses now and doing well. Some programs will admit students on a provisional basis; in other words, on the condition that they make up for deficiencies in preparation or performance or achieve a certain grade point average in the first semester.

For example, Cindy Liutkus took additional undergraduate courses when the four graduate programs in geology in which she was interested indicated she was deficient in chemistry and mathematics. "After talking with the chairs of the various departments," says Liutkus, "I decided to take two summer courses at a local college to make up for my weaknesses in chemistry and math. Many departments stated that it shows a great deal of drive and dedication if a student is willing to take the initiative to strengthen areas of weakness by doing summer sessions. It definitely paid off for me." With the additional courses under her belt, Liutkus gained admission to her first choice. Jenn Wagaman had a similar experience when she applied to the master's program in public communications at the University of Alaska at Fairbanks. As an undergraduate, she had majored in anthropology and minored in art.

In addition, her GRE scores were low. So to bring her qualifications up to par, Wagaman spent a semester taking undergraduate journalism courses and preparing to take the GRE a second time. With her additional course work and improved GRE scores, Wagaman was admitted to the program.

Internships and Placement

If professional practice is an important component of the degree you are seeking, be sure to investigate what internships are available to students. This is an important consideration for people in clinical psychology, social work, counseling, or any other field for which the degree is preparation for practice in the field. The contacts you make while doing internships can be valuable to you when you look for a job after graduation. Felecia Bartow, who is interested in international social development, looked for the availability of international internships when she was narrowing her selection of social work programs.

Most important, find out what services are available to help you find suitable employment once you receive your degree. What is the program's track record in finding its graduates positions? Does the university offer career development services, like a centralized office that will send out your credentials to prospective employers?

What happens to graduates of the program? What types of jobs do they get? If you are looking at Ph.D. programs and hope eventually to teach and do research at the university level, it is especially important to find out whether recent graduates have been able to find academic positions. Are they in tenure-track positions at reputable departments, or do they go from one temporary appointment to another? What percentage of graduates takes jobs in business, industry, government agencies, or nonprofits? You want to have a good idea, at the outset, of your employment prospects as a graduate of this program.

Size and Diversity

Are you interested in a large program or a small program? There are pros and cons to each type of experience. Large programs may offer a wide variety of specialists, but they may not always provide the personal attention that small programs can. When searching for master's programs in communications, size was important to Andrea Edwards Myers. "I wanted the luxury of attending small classes with one-on-one instruction if I needed it. A big university program would not have suited my needs." However, keep in mind that small programs may have limitations and weaknesses in some areas of research.

In addition, you should consider the number of graduate students in the program. It may be helpful to have a critical mass of fellow students to help you absorb all the new material you will be learning. According to Cindy Liutkus, a Ph.D. candidate in geology at Rutgers University in New Jersey, "I always found it beneficial to have other students who are interested in your area so that you can discuss topics of interest, bounce ideas around, and get help with interpretations and tough predicaments."

The diversity of the students and faculty members may be a consideration as well. If you are an international or minority student, are there other students or a local community with your background? If you are very religious, very liberal, very conservative, or very anything else, will you feel comfortable with the politics and values of the program and the surrounding community?

> Even if you are pursuing an academic degree, such as a Ph.D. in anthopology or history, check whether the program offers internships. Some academic programs are beginning to add internships to their offerings in an attempt to broaden the employment prospects of their students.

To Melany Kahn, the variety of people in New York University's film program was a plus. "Because NYU gets so many applications, it has the luxury of choosing interesting, diverse classes. For example, I was the only student from New York City in my class of 38 people. We had thirteen countries represented in our year alone," says Kahn.

Last, but not least, you can learn a great deal from a program's retention rate. Of the individuals who begin their studies there, how many drop out and why? How many transfer to other programs? How many are asked to leave? If a program has a below-average retention rate, you should be asking why.

Full-Time or Part-Time?

In most academic Ph.D. programs as well as many health-care programs, full-time study is the only option. However, many other programs admit part-time students or allow a portion of the requirements to be completed on a part-time basis. Professional schools are more likely to allow part-time study because many of their students work full-time in the field and are pursuing the degree to improve their career opportunities. For many people, working full-time and studying part-time is the only way to make graduate education affordable.

If you are thinking of pursuing an academic master's program on a part-time basis, you should be aware of the possible disadvantages. In spite of the fact that more and more students are pursuing graduate education on a part-time basis, they often find that they are not taken seriously in the academic community. Because they are not committing all of their time to their studies, part-time students are often considered less dedicated. Professors can be impatient with their limited study time and work obligations and may not make the extra effort to schedule office hours, field work, and other things at times convenient for part-time students. On the other hand, a program may be making efforts to accommodate part-time students' schedules through e-mail and course Web sites. Be sure to find out what the attitude toward part-time students is in the programs you are researching.

If you are considering part-time graduate programs, you should evaluate them on the same basis as you would evaluate full-time programs. Are the admissions standards the same for both part- and

> You can learn a great deal from a program's retention rate. If a program has a below-average retention rate, you should be asking why.

full-time students? If they are not, the part-time program may not be up to the standards of the full-time program. Do the same faculty members teach night or weekend classes as those who teach day classes, or are less qualified instructors assigned to less traditional schedules? In addition, there are some practical things you should check. Are classes scheduled at times that are convenient for you? Are libraries, bookstores, student services, and other facilities open at times you can use them?

On-Campus Program or Distance Learning Program?

Again, to pursue a graduate degree in an academic discipline, the traditional on-campus program is almost the only option available. But for those pursuing career-oriented degrees, there are two reasons to consider distance learning programs. The first is location—you can be far from the campus on which the course work originates. The second is time—some, but not all, distance learning programs offer the opportunity to do course work at your own convenience, even in the wee hours of the morning. So for people with work and family schedules that cannot accommodate regular part-time weekend or evening classes, the flexibility of some distance learning programs may be ideal.

For example, with an online Internet-based program, you can do most of your course work at any time of day or night—even at 3 a.m. Kim Foreman, who works full-time as Administrative Director of Quality/Resource and Risk Management at Hackettstown Community Hospital in New Jersey and has a family, began her search for master's programs in health-care administration by looking at part-time and executive weekend programs. "Traditional on-campus evening classes interfered with work and family obligations. The weekend programs still required that I be at a certain place at a certain time, and this was also inconvenient," says Foreman. "I wanted flexibility and a program that allowed me to be self-directed but still have interaction with faculty and classmates." Foreman is now a master's candidate in Seton Hall

University's online Master of Health-care Administration program. Courses are conducted over the Internet, with faculty members, visiting scholars, and students using bulletin-board technology to conduct seminars over time.

Flexibility was an important factor for Laurie Noe, too. Noe, an Ed.D. candidate in management of children and youth programs at Nova Southeastern University, based in Florida, found that distance learning programs offered her the ability to do course work on her own schedule. Noe, who directs a large early childhood center in Connecticut and has a family, explains, "I wanted a distance program that would give me the flexibility to pace myself with just enough physical contact and deadlines to motivate me." Monthly regional meetings and an annual conference in Florida help create social bonds among the students and faculty members.

A word of warning about the current reputation of distance learning in the traditional academic community. Some view distance learning programs as the modern equivalent of the old matchbook diploma mills. And some programs are, no doubt, of dubious quality. But as technology improves, the Internet continues to change the way we communicate, and more reputable universities begin to establish distance learning programs, this type of education will begin to be viewed as more mainstream. However, we are not yet at that point. Therefore, when you investigate a distance learning program, be sure you subject it to a thorough evaluation; you don't want to wind up with an inferior degree.

Ed Goldberg, the Chief Executive of SetonWorldwide, Seton Hall University's online degree programs, advises prospective students to consider four factors when evaluating a distance learning program:

• Credibility

Is the program accredited by the appropriate regional and specialized organizations? Are the faculty members primarily full-time tenured professors or adjuncts? Does the program make full use of technology to bring scholars and practitioners from around the world into the classroom?

• Content

Does the program's content match your educational goals? Is the curriculum up to date? For example, is e-commerce part of a business degree curriculum? Is the program rigorous? How much time are you expected to spend on course work? What are the requirements for the degree? Time on task and requirements should be on a par with traditional degree programs.

• Flexibility

Some distance learning programs offer real-time instruction. That means you must be at a certain place at a certain time to receive instruction. Others, like the online program in which Foreman is enrolled, offer asynchronous instruction by means of course bulletin boards on the Internet. That means that you can log on any time and any place to do your course work.

• Instructional design

What does the program do to overcome the inherent isolation of a student in a distance learning program? Some programs depend on regular face-to-face meetings to forge a learning community. Others use the cohort method, in which a group starts a program together and stays together until the degree is completed. Is the instructional design passive or active? Are you on the receiving end of lectures and respond only through papers and exams, or is there seminar-style interaction between faculty members and students and among students?

Time to Degree

How long does it take the average student to complete the degree, and what time limits does the program set? Do Ph.D. candidates enter a twilight zone while they write their dissertations, or do they usually finish in a timely manner? The average time to complete a Ph.D. degree varies from discipline to discipline, but if you check several programs, you will at least be able to compare their statistics. If average time to degree is not mentioned in the information packet and it's something that concerns you, call the program to find out.

Time to degree can also be an important consideration for people who don't want a graduate program to go on indefinitely. For example, one thing that appealed to Bob Connelly about Seton Hall University's executive doctoral program in educational administration was its tight timeline. Connelly, who is superintendent of schools for Delaware Township, New Jersey, explains, "The program was highly structured and had distinct timetables....It imposed a schedule that would not allow procrastination. For example, I had to propose a dissertation topic on the very first day. The topic may not have been completely realistic, but having to come up with it got me started."

Another factor you may need to consider is whether there is a maximum time to complete a degree; in other words, a deadline. Some programs set a cap on the number of years you can matriculate; in other words, be officially enrolled as a student working on a degree. If you are planning on getting the degree on a part-time basis, you should be sure to check whether there is a deadline that is realistic for your needs.

To Andrea Edwards Myers, a full-time editor with a family, not having a deadline by which to finish her master's degree was one factor in favor of the public communications program at the College of St. Rose in Albany, New York. "The program is offered on a part-time evening basis and there is no timeline for completion," explains Myers. "The fact that it will take me four years to complete the thirty-six credit hours works well for me."

Location

Location is often a big factor when you are selecting programs; in fact, it's the most important factor to students who, for personal reasons, are unwilling to move and are not interested in distance learning programs. However, there are other issues related to location that you may also want to consider. How close is the program to other institutions with which you may be collaborating? If you are a field scientist, how close is the program to your field areas? If you will need to do research elsewhere or are an international student, is the program conveniently located for travel?

Cost and Likelihood of Getting Funding

Tuition and fees can range from a couple of thousand dollars a year for state residents at public institutions to more than $25,000 a year at top private colleges and universities. Add to that your living expenses, and the annual costs can be considerable if you are attending school full-time. For some people, the cost differential between public and private institutions is large enough to be an important factor when selecting programs, especially at the master's level where funding is less common and the degree itself, rather than the program, may be more important. If you are considering programs at public institutions in other states, find out what's involved in establishing residency and qualifying for lower tuition and fees.

Keep in mind that when a department has funding to award its graduate students, Ph.D. candidates are more likely to receive help than master's candidates, and full-time students are more likely to receive help than part-time students. In addition, large research institutions with national reputations usually have more resources with which to help students than smaller, regional institutions. Of course, if you are working, your annual costs will be lower because you'll be taking only one or two courses at a time. In addition, your employer may help with full or partial tuition reimbursement. We'll discuss sources of funding more fully in Chapter 8.

The University Environment

In addition to evaluating factors specific to a department or program, look at the college or university as a whole. We've already discussed the issue of reputation, but there is more to consider. What facilities, including libraries, labs, and computers, are available to students? What is the quality of those facilities? Are library collections large and up to date?

What support services does the university offer students? Is university housing available to graduate students and their families? Can you use career development resources even if you are a part-time student? If you are an international student, what administrative and social support can you expect to find? What is your impression of the administrators with whom you have had interactions? Is the institution

"You're going to be in a college town for a while, usually with dwindling finances. Don't forget to pick a living environment in which you can stand to be broke."

impersonal in its dealings, or do the staff members do their best for each student? Felecia Bartow recalls that the Dean of Admissions at Washington University addressed her questions personally and remembered who she was. "This personal touch," says Bartow, "proved to be indicative of the general quality of both faculty and staff members at the school."

In addition to your impressions of the university staff, consider the campus environment. Is it the only major institution in a small college town or one urban campus among several in a big city? If you are accustomed to small towns and campuses, will you be comfortable with a large urban university? Is the cost of living high or low? Although to Neill Kipp, a Ph.D. candidate in computer science at Virginia Tech, the faculty was the most important consideration when he was looking at graduate programs, but he also put the campus environment high on his list. "You're going to be in a college town for a while, usually with dwindling finances. Don't forget to pick a living environment in which you can stand to be broke." If you have a family, does the university and local community provide decent housing, good employment opportunities for your spouse, and quality day care or a good school system for your children?

YOUR PERSONAL CHECKLIST

This chapter discusses a dozen factors that you can consider when evaluating a graduate program. In the end, however, there may be only three or four aspects of a program that really concern you. That is why the self-assessment you did at the very start is so crucial, since you can now focus on what's important to you when you are evaluating programs (see Appendix 1 for a program selection checklist).

Like Heather Helms-Erikson, a Ph.D. candidate in human development and family studies at Penn State, you may put faculty mentoring and program reputation at the top of the list. Or, like Naaz Qureshi, an M.B.A. student at Southern Methodist University in Dallas, you may think that location and diversity are very important factors. According to Qureshi, "Nonacademic factors played a large part in my decision. I needed to like the city where I would be spending the next two years, and I wanted a program with a diverse student body."

You may have work and family commitments that will strongly influence your choices. For example, Kim Foreman needed a program that was compatible with her lifestyle. "For me, flexibility of my time had to be addressed. I balance a busy work schedule (with a long commute) with an active family life (young children at home and, at times, a traveling husband). I needed a program that would allow me to go to school when I had time, and that would change on a daily basis! The online distance learning program was just what I needed."

If you keep your own needs in the forefront during the selection process, you should be able to narrow your choices appropriately. As Jim Lipuma, a Ph.D. candidate in environmental science from New Jersey Institute of Technology concludes, "Every person and every program is different. If you search long and hard enough, you can find the program for you."

Taking Graduate Admissions Tests

For some applicants, the prospect of taking one of the graduate admissions tests is enough to make them put aside their graduate school plans indefinitely. You may be anxious about taking the Graduate Record Examination (GRE) or one of the professional exams, but usually there is no way of avoiding it. Most programs require one of the major standardized exams and they may also require a subject area test, writing assessment, or test of English language proficiency if you are not a native speaker of English. So unless you've selected programs that do not require an examination, you are going to have to take an exam—and do well.

The first thing you should do is determine which exam(s), if any, you are expected to take. This information should appear in the packet that accompanies the program's application form. If you do not yet have this material, you should simply call the admissions office or program and ask. Once you know which exam you must take, contact the testing service that administers the exam and request registration materials or register on line. Information on contacting the testing services appears in Appendix 2.

Before we go into detail about the tests, it might be helpful to discuss how an admissions committee might use your score. The role played by a graduate admissions test is similar to the one played by the SAT I or ACT on the undergraduate level. It provides a benchmark. Essentially, it is the one of the few objective bits of information in your application that can be used to gauge where you fall in the range of applicants. Some programs, especially the top professional programs that receive many more applicants than they can admit, may use the score as a means of reducing the applicant pool: if your score is below their cutoff, they will not even look at the rest of your application. But most programs are much more flexible in the way they evaluate scores. If your score is low, you may still be considered for admission, especially if your grade point average is high or your application is otherwise strong.

But let's face it—a low or average score will not help your case. When Heather Helms-Erikson applied to master's degree programs in marriage and family therapy, she took the GRE with no preparation during finals week. "I did well enough to get in but not well enough to get funding," she says. A few years later, when applying to Ph.D. programs in human development and family studies, Helms-Erikson was determined to get the best funding package she could. To that end, she studied 2 to 5 hours a week for four months preparing for the GRE. Needless to say, her score was considerably higher—and she was admitted to several programs with funding.

One story does not prove that a good score will open all doors. But you should regard the test as an opportunity to improve your application. And that means you must take the test in plenty of time to meet application deadlines. That way, if you take the test early and are disappointed with the results, you will have time to retake it.

You must also prepare. Thorough preparation can add points to your score by refreshing your memory and giving you practice with test taking. Preparation is especially important for applicants who have been out of school for years. You may need to do a quick recap of high school mathematics, for example, to do well on the mathematics portion of the test. And you may have forgotten what test taking is like. Study and practice will help you overcome any weaknesses you may have. We'll discuss ways to prepare for the exams later in the chapter after we describe the various tests.

> Be sure to take standardized tests well in advance of your application deadlines. This gives you a chance to take the test again if you want to improve your score.

THE GRADUATE RECORD EXAMINATIONS

There are three types of Graduate Record Examinations: the General Test, which is usually referred to as the GRE; the subject tests; and the Writing Assessment. Each of these tests has a different purpose and you may need to take more than one of them. If so, try not to schedule two tests on the same day. The experience may be more arduous than you anticipate.

The General Test (GRE)

According to the Educational Testing Service, the GRE "measures verbal, quantitative, and analytical reasoning skills that have been developed over a long period of time and are not necessarily related to any field of study." Like the SAT, the GRE is a test designed to assess whether you have the aptitude for higher-level study. Even though the GRE may not have subject area relevance, it can indicate that you are capable of doing the difficult reading, synthesizing, and writing demanded of most graduate students.

The GRE is a computer-adaptive test. It is divided into three separately timed parts, and all the questions are multiple-choice: (1) a 30-minute verbal section consisting of 30 questions; (2) a 45-minute quantitative section with 28 questions; and (3) a 60-minute analytical section of 35 questions. The parts may be presented in any order. In addition, an unidentified verbal, quantitative, or analytical section that doesn't count toward your score may be included. You don't have any way to tell which of the duplicated sections is the "real" one, so you should complete both carefully. Finally, another section on which ETS is still doing research may also appear. This section will be identified as such and will also not count toward your score. ETS informs test takers on planning to spend about four and a half hours at the testing site.

Verbal Section

The thirty questions in the verbal section of the GRE test your ability to recognize relationships between words and concepts, analyze sentences, and analyze and evaluate written material. In other words, they test your vocabulary and your reading and thinking skills. There are four main types of questions.

- In sentence completion questions, sentences are presented with a missing word(s). You are asked to select the words that best complete the sentences. Answering correctly involves figuring out the meanings of the missing words from their context in the sentence.

- Analogy questions present a pair of words or phrases that are related to one another. Your task is to figure out the relationship between the two words or phrases. Then you must select the pair of words or phrases whose relationship is most similar to that of the given pair.
- In antonym questions, you are given a word and asked to select the word that is most opposite in meaning.
- Reading comprehension questions test your ability to understand a reading passage and synthesize information on the basis of what you've read.

The words and reading material on which you are tested in this section come from a wide range of subjects, ranging from daily life to the sciences and humanities.

Quantitative Section

This section of the GRE tests your basic mathematical skills and your understanding of elementary mathematical concepts. You will be tested on your ability to reason quantitatively and solve quantitative problems.

- Quantitative comparison questions require that you determine which of two quantities is the larger, if possible. If such a determination is not possible, then you must so indicate.
- Data analysis questions provide you with a graph or a table on which to base your solution to a problem.
- Problem-solving questions test a variety of mathematical concepts. They may be word problems or symbolic problems.

The quantitative questions test your knowledge of arithmetic and high school algebra, geometry, and data analysis. They do not cover trigonometry or calculus.

Analytical Section

According to the ETS, the analytical section of the GRE "tests your ability to understand structured sets of relationships, deduce new information from sets of relationships, analyze and evaluate arguments,

Given that the GRE and GMAT are only given in computer-based format, it might be a good idea to do at least some preparation using test preparation software. Using print materials exclusively may mean that you are inadequately prepared for some aspects of the computer-based test.

identify central issues and hypotheses, draw sound inferences, and identify plausible causal relationships." In other words, can you reason analytically and logically? There are two main types of questions in this section:

- Analytical reasoning questions appear in groups, and they are all based on the same set of conditions or rules. A situation is described and you are told how many people or things you will be manipulating. Then you are asked to manipulate the items according to the conditions. For example, you may be given information about a group of people and then asked to rank them in order of age.
- Logical reasoning questions consist of arguments that you must analyze and evaluate. Each argument has assumptions, facts, and conclusions, and you must answer questions that test your ability to assess these.

The subject matter in the analytical section is drawn from all fields of study as well as everyday life.

Computer-Adaptive Tests

The GRE is now given only in computer format, and the test is somewhat different from the old paper-and-pencil test. At the start of each section, you are given questions of moderate difficulty. The computer uses your responses to each question and its knowledge of the test's structure to decide which question to give you next. If your responses continue to be correct, how does the computer reward you? It gives you a harder question. On the other hand, if you answer incorrectly, the next question will typically be easier. In short, the computer uses a cumulative assessment of your performance along with information about the test's design to decide which question you get next.

One result of this format is that you cannot skip a question. The computer needs your answer to a question before it can give you the next one. So you have no choice. You must answer or you get a "no score." In addition, this format means you cannot go back to a previous question to change your answer. The computer has already taken your

> On computer-adaptive tests, each person's test is different. Even if two people start with the same item set in the basic test section, once they differ on an answer, the subsequent portion of the test will branch differently.

answer and used it to give you subsequent questions. No backtracking is possible once you've entered and confirmed your answer.

According to the ETS, even though people take different tests, their scores are comparable. This is because the characteristics of the questions answered correctly and incorrectly, including their difficulty levels, are taken into account in the calculation of the score. In addition, ETS claims that the computer-based test scores are also comparable to the old paper-and-pencil test scores.

One benefit of the computer-based format is that when you finish, you can cancel the test results—before seeing them—if you feel you've done poorly. If you do decide to keep the test, then you can see your unofficial scores right away. In addition, official score reporting is relatively fast—ten to fifteen days.

A drawback of the format, besides the fact that you cannot skip around, is that some of the readings, graphs, and questions are too large to appear on the screen in their entirety. You have to scroll up and down to see the whole item. Likewise, referring back to a passage or graph while answering a question means that you must scroll up. In addition, you can't underline sentences in a passage or make marks in the margin as you could on the paper test. To make up for this, ETS provides scratch paper that you can use to make notes and do calculations.

To help test-takers accustom themselves to the computerized format, ETS provides a tutorial that you complete before starting on the actual test. The tutorial familiarizes you with the use of a mouse, the conventions of pointing, clicking, scrolling, and the format of the test. If you are familiar with computers, the tutorial will take you less than half an hour. If you are not, you are permitted to spend more time on it. According to ETS, the system is easy to use, even for a person with no previous computer experience. However, if you are not accustomed to computers you would be far better off to practice your basic skills before you get to the testing site. Although in theory a mouse is easy to use, novices often have trouble getting the cursor to go where they want it to go. The last thing you want to deal with while taking the GRE is a wild mouse and accidental clicking on the wrong answers. If it's any consolation, no knowledge of the keyboard is required—everything is accomplished by pointing and clicking.

Subject Area Tests

The subject area tests are achievement tests, and they test your content knowledge of a particular subject. There are fourteen subject area tests at present, and they are given in paper-and-pencil format only. The subjects include biochemistry and cell and molecular biology, biology, chemistry, computer science, economics, engineering, geology, history, literature in English, mathematics, music, physics, psychology, and sociology, although history and sociology will soon be discontinued. The subject area tests assume a level of knowledge consistent with majoring in a subject or at least having an extensive background in it. ETS suggests allowing about three and a half hours at the testing site when taking a subject area test.

Unlike the General Test, which is given many times all year round, the subject tests are given only three times a year. Keep in mind that because the tests are paper-based, it takes four to six weeks for your scores to be mailed to your designated institutions. Because the tests are given infrequently and score reporting is slow, be sure you plan ahead carefully so your test results will arrive before your deadlines.

The Writing Assessment

Introduced in 1999, the Writing Assessment is a performance-based assessment of critical reasoning skills and analytical writing. It can be taken in computer or paper formats and consists of two parts:

- In the 45-minute "Present Your Perspective on an Issue" task, you must address an issue from any point of view and provide examples and reasons to explain and support your perspective. You are given a choice of two essay topics.
- In the 30-minute "Analyze an Argument" task, you must critique an argument by telling how well reasoned it is. There is no choice of topics in this section.

Scoring of the Writing Assessment is done according to a seven-point scale (0 is the worst; 6 is the best) by college and university faculty members with experience in teaching writing or writing-intensive courses. Each essay is scored independently by two readers. If the two scores are not identical or adjacent, a third reader will be used. The reported score is the average of your two essay scores. If you think the score is unfair, you may request a rescoring.

MILLER ANALOGIES TEST

The Miller Analogies Test (MAT), which is administered by the Psychological Corporation, is accepted by more than 2,300 graduate school programs. It is a test of mental ability given entirely in the form of analogies. The MAT tests your "store" of general information on a variety of subjects through the different types of analogies you must complete. For example, the analogies may tap your knowledge of fine arts, literature, mathematics, natural science, and social science.

On the MAT, you have 50 minutes to solve 100 problems. The test is given on an as-needed basis at more than 600 test centers in the United States.

PROFESSIONAL SCHOOL EXAMS

Professional graduate programs are likely to require you to take the appropriate graduate admissions test. The major tests are the Graduate Management Admissions Test (GMAT), for business school applicants; the Law School Admissions Test (LSAT), for law school applicants; and the Medical College Admissions Test (MCAT), for medical school applicants. However, there are also specialized graduate admissions tests in the fields of dentistry, veterinary science, pharmacy, optometry, and education. Information on contacting the various testing agencies for these exams is given in Appendix 2.

Graduate Management Admissions Test

Like the GRE, the GMAT is a computer-adaptive test designed to help schools of business assess applicants' aptitude for graduate level programs in business and management. It is run by the Graduate Management Admissions Council and administered by ETS.

The GMAT tests verbal, quantitative, and analytic writing skills. In the verbal section, you will be asked to understand and evaluate standard written English. The quantitative section tests your basic math skills, understanding of elementary mathematical concepts, and ability to solve quantitative problems. The writing section measures your ability to think critically and communicate in writing.

Law School Admissions Test

There are about 200 members of the Law School Admissions Council and they all require their applicants to take the LSAT, which is given a couple of times a year. The LSAT has five 35-minute sections, all multiple-choice; four of the five multiple-choice sections are counted toward your score. The fifth section is intended to pretest new test items. The LSAT also has a 30-minute writing section.

The scored multiple-choice portion of the test includes one reading comprehension section, one analytical reasoning section, and two logical reasoning sections. At the end of the test is the writing sample, which is not scored. Instead, a copy of your writing sample is sent to each school to which you apply.

Medical College Admissions Test

The MCAT combines features of an achievement test and an aptitude test. It tests your knowledge of basic concepts in biology, chemistry, and physics as well as your ability to think critically, solve scientific problems, and write. For premedical students, this test provokes a lot of anxiety—and for good reason. Medical schools use the scores to reduce their applicant pools, so doing well is important.

You get four scores on the MCAT. The three multiple-choice portions of the test—verbal reasoning, physical sciences, and biological sciences—are scored on a scale from 1 to 15. The writing sample, which consists of two essays, has a separate score, from J (low) to T (high). Since the test is given only twice a year and you need time to study, you should plan your test dates well in advance.

TESTS OF ENGLISH LANGUAGE PROFICIENCY

If your native language is not English, you may be required to take the Test of English as a Foreign Language (TOEFL) or Test of Spoken English (TSE) in order to determine your proficiency in English. Both tests are administered by ETS.

The TOEFL is given in computer-based form throughout most of the world. Like the computer-based GRE, the TOEFL does not require previous computer experience. You are given the opportunity to practice on the computer before the test begins. The TOEFL has four sections—listening, reading, structure, and writing—and it lasts about 4 hours.

The TSE evaluates your ability to speak English. During the test, which takes about half an hour, you answer questions that are presented in written and recorded form. Your responses are tape recorded; there is no writing required on this test. The TSE is not given in as many locations as the TOEFL, so you may have to travel a considerable distance to take it.

PREPARING FOR THE TESTS

You can improve your scores and reduce your test anxiety by preparing for the exams you need to take. At the very least, preparation will mean that you are familiar with the test instructions and the types of questions you will be asked. If your computer skills need improvement, adequate preparation will mean you can focus on the questions rather than struggle with the mouse when you take the computer-based tests. For achievement tests such as the subject area tests and the MCAT, you will actually need to study content. There are many ways you can prepare for the tests, but whichever method you choose, start early. (For a list of test preparation resources, see Appendix 2.)

Jim Lipuma, who is earning a Ph.D. in environmental science at New Jersey Institute of Technology, favored practice tests. "My only advice for the tests is to read and practice with old tests...Though I did not use a review course or 'study,' I did know exactly what to expect by reviewing sample exams...Cramming will not work for more than a few points. Others I know who have also done well have pretested using old tests to hone skills." You can check the Web sites of the various tests to download or request practice tests, or you can buy practice test books at a bookstore.

Other students used workbooks that give information and test-taking strategies as well as practice items. Bob Connelly, who earned an

Ed.D. in educational administration from Seton Hall University in New Jersey, used a workbook to prepare for the MAT. "I'm glad I did," says Connelly. "If I had gone in cold, I would not have recognized the patterns of the analogies, and the test would have been more stressful." There are many workbooks, some with CD-ROMs, that will help you prepare for a graduate admissions test.

Many students don't trust themselves to stick with a self-study program using practice tests, workbooks, or software. If this sounds like you, you may prefer the structure and discipline of a professional review course. Although the courses are much more expensive than the do-it-yourself approach, they may be worth it if they make you study. "I found it was extremely helpful to take a prep course before taking the GMAT," says Naaz Qureshi, an M.B.A. candidate at the Cox School of Business at Southern Methodist University. "The classes got me in the mindset of how to approach the questions rather than simply answering them based on my best educated guess."

Another test preparation resource is your college professors. If you are still in college, you can ask your professors if they would be willing to help you and other students prepare for the MCAT or a subject area test. At Bucknell University, Cindy Liutkus's undergraduate professors actually gave a workshop for students preparing for the geology test. Each professor gave a half-hour lecture that touched on the major points the students should remember. Liutkus also asked her professors for a syllabus of the important topics that they covered in each of their courses to guide her studying.

RETAKING THE TESTS

As they say, practice makes perfect. One way to improve your scores is to take the test more than once. Luis De la Cruz, who is studying for his M.B.A. at Worcester Polytechnic Institute in Massachusetts, took the GMAT three times. "It is important not to get discouraged by an unfavorable score," says De la Cruz. "You can always improve your score."

Some programs will admit you conditionally despite a poor score, but they expect you to retake the test and improve your performance.

One applicant from Italy missed a question on the TSE, lowering her score to 220 (out of 300), which was 10 points below the cutoff for the program to which she was applying. She was admitted on a conditional basis and when she retook the test, she scored 300. When applying to the public communications program at the University of Alaska in Fairbanks, Jenn Wagaman had a similar experience with the GRE. "I took the GRE the first time when I was living in my hometown of New Orleans. I did miserably," says Wagaman. "I was lucky enough to be admitted to a graduate program at a small school that knew my capabilities and was willing to let me take another stab at my scores." The second time she took the GRE, Wagaman's scores went up 300 points.

REDUCING TEST ANXIETY

The best way to reduce test anxiety is to be thoroughly prepared. If you are well-acquainted with the format, directions, and types of questions you will encounter, you will not need to waste precious test time puzzling over these aspects of the exam. In addition to thorough preparation, here are some suggestions to reduce the stress of taking the exam.

The best way to reduce anxiety is to be thoroughly prepared.

- Get a good night's rest and don't tank up on caffeinated beverages. They will only make you feel more stressed.
- Make sure you've got all the things you will need, including your admission, ticket proper identification, and pencils and erasers if you are taking a paper-based test.
- Dress in layers so you will be prepared for a range of room temperatures.
- Get to the testing site at least a half an hour early. Make sure you know the way and leave yourself plenty of time to get there.
- Pace yourself during the exam. It is to your benefit to answer each question and complete each section.

Finally, try to keep things in perspective. The exam is just one part of a much larger application process, as we'll discuss in the next chapter.

Applying

Now that you have narrowed your selection of graduate programs, it's time to prepare and assemble your applications. If you have not already done so, request an application and information packet from each program to which you plan to apply. When you look over these materials, you will see that there is a lot of work involved in applying to graduate school. It may take you a year or more to assemble and submit all the necessary information, especially if you're an international student or you've been out of school for a few years. Because the process is complicated and time consuming, you should start well in advance.

TIMETABLE

In general, it's advisable to start the application process at least a year and a half before you plan to enroll. Allow yourself even more time if you are applying for national fellowships or if you are applying to a health-care program through your college's evaluation committee. In these cases, you may need to start two years before matriculation in order to meet all of the deadlines for test scores, letters of recommendation, and so on.

Application deadlines for fall admission may range from August—one full year prior to your planned enrollment—to late spring or summer for programs with rolling admissions. However, most programs require that you submit your application between January and March of the year in which you wish to start. Be careful when you check the deadlines in the application packet. Different programs at the same university may have different deadlines.

In addition, if you are applying for financial aid, you should leave yourself extra time to assemble all of the financial information you'll need to support your request for assistance. Applicants for aid usually have to send in the entire application by an earlier date than the deadline for those not seeking aid. Be certain that you understand

**"Deadlines are
really important if
you want to get
funding. You may
be highly qualified
but lose out if you
miss a deadline."**

which deadline applies to you. After all, what's the point of being admitted if you cannot afford to attend?

It's usually advantageous to apply early if you can. For one thing, an early application demonstrates strong interest and motivation on your part, especially when a program uses rolling admissions. Even more important, however, applying early means that the department or program will evaluate your application when it still has a full budget of funding to award. When you apply late, you may not be awarded full or even partial funding because the department has already used up its resources. "Deadlines are really important if you want to get funding," says Suzette Vandeburg, Assistant Vice Provost for Graduate Studies at the State University of New York at Binghamton. "You may be highly qualified but lose out if you miss a deadline."

This does not mean that you will necessarily miss out on funding if you just squeeze in by the program's deadline, but given the competition for financial aid, why gamble? While you could get lucky, you may be in for some weeks of nail biting until a program makes all of its awards. "When I applied to graduate school, I noticed that many positions were offered early, especially in departments that were very small and very competitive," says Cindy Liutkus, a Ph.D. candidate in geology at Rutgers University in New Jersey. "Because I hadn't applied as early as most people, I had to wait until two of the departments obtained rejections from their early offers before I knew whether I would receive a teaching assistantship or a research assistantship." Still, you shouldn't rely on luck for something so important. Apply early. You can use the timeline in Appendix 1 to help you plan the application process.

WHAT HAPPENS TO YOUR APPLICATION?

Before we discuss the elements of an application, it will be helpful for you to understand what happens to your application once you submit it. In general, your application is handled first by an admissions office and then by the admissions committee that makes the decisions.

The Role of the Admissions Office

If you are applying to an academic program that is part of a university, you will be sending your application to a centralized graduate studies admissions office. This office is responsible for establishing your file and coordinating all of the activity related to your application. As parts of your application arrive, an admissions staff member places each item in your file and records its receipt. In a well-run office, the staff will also notify you if anything is missing. Once your application is complete, the admissions office forwards a copy of it to the department or program's admissions committee for evaluation and recommendation.

University graduate admissions offices usually act as clearing-houses for applications, but in some cases they have the authority to reject an applicant or to waive a university requirement for an exceptional candidate. For example, they can turn down an applicant whose qualifications are clearly below university standard (e.g., someone with an extremely low GPA for all four college years). They can also bar an application from further consideration if it is incomplete.

Applications to professional schools generally go directly to the professional school's admissions office. The admissions office in a professional school coordinates the application process, but, unlike the centralized university admissions office, it also takes an active role in the evaluation and decision-making process. The admissions committee of a professional school usually consists of representatives from the admissions office as well as faculty members.

The Role of the Admissions Committee

The members of the admissions committee are the people on whom your future depends. They are the small group of department or program faculty members and administrators who review and evaluate each applicant and decide not only who gets in, but who gets funding. Admissions committees usually have at least four sources of information on which to base their decision about your application: your transcripts, your test scores, your personal essay, and your letters of recommendation. The importance of each of these sources will vary from admissions committee to admissions committee and also, will vary among the members of a committee. Their decision making processes will vary as well. Let's take a look at how three actual admissions committees work to give you an idea of what goes on behind closed doors.

A Program in the Social Sciences

The admissions committee for this program receives about 120 applications per year. A staff member extracts certain data, including undergraduate school attended, degree earned, and area of concentration; grade point average; GRE scores; and field of interest. This information is placed on a cover sheet and attached to the application. This cover sheet is the first thing the admissions committee members will see when they pick up an application.

A few weeks after the application deadline, the committee meets for a day-long marathon of reading and assessing applications. The applications are divided into two groups—master's degree candidates and doctoral degree candidates—and are handled separately. Each application is passed around for each committee member to read. While the applicant's essay and letters of recommendation are fresh in each person's mind, the committee makes a decision on the candidate.

Usually, there is agreement on the acceptance or rejection of an applicant, but occasionally members of the committee have a difference of opinion on a particular candidate. In that case, if no one is willing to back down, a decision on the candidate may be deferred until the candidate can be interviewed. Or the candidate may be accepted on a conditional basis. At the same time that the accept/reject decision is being made, a tentative decision on department funding is also made. After all of the applications have been evaluated, the committee goes through the applications in the acceptance pile again, adjusting the funding decisions that they made on the first round.

In this committee, a great deal of weight is placed on the personal essay. Members of the committee are looking for evidence that a candidate is focused and committed. "We look to see whether the applicant knows why he or she is applying to our graduate program in a specific way, not just as a next step in life while they're figuring out what to do," comments one member of the committee. "When a student knows what our strengths are, and how their interests fit into our program, we are impressed."

A Program in the Hard Sciences

In this department, the admissions committee consists of five faculty members, one from each major division of the department. Each faculty member reviews the applications of the students interested in his or her area of specialization. In addition, the chair of the committee reviews all the applications. Periodically, the committee meets to discuss and make decisions on the applicants. Since the department has the resources to fund all first-year students, an acceptance automatically means the student will have financial support.

In this committee, grade point average and letters of recommendation are weighted heavily. A minimum GPA of 3.0 is required, although extenuating circumstances are considered if the GPA is uneven; a typical example is a low freshman year GPA, which the committee may decide to overlook. The letters of recommendation are important because the committee learns about the student's undergraduate research experience and relevant summer internships from them. Of the four main elements of the application, the essay is the least important to this committee. As long as it is coherent and gives an indication of the student's interest in research, the members pay little further attention to it.

This particular committee does not try to make a match between every single applicant and a faculty member with similar research interests. "Students often change their minds once they get here," comments a member of the committee. This is unlike other programs, where the admissions committees may turn down an excellent applicant solely because there is no faculty member to work with the student. In other words, if there is no faculty member who shares the student's area of interest and wants to work with him or her, the applicant will be rejected.

An M.B.A. Program

The admissions committee of this M.B.A. program operates quite differently from the two admissions committees we've already discussed. First, the committee is comprised of three members from the program's admissions office; the associate dean, who is also a faculty member; and a representative from the career development office.

> Close to half of all business school applications are reviewed by students currently in the program.

Each application is read at least twice. The first reading is conducted by current M.B.A. students, which is typical of the admissions process in 40 to 50 percent of business schools. The student readers are looking for minimum academic achievement as reflected by GPA and GMAT scores, but more importantly, they are looking for evidence that the applicant has strong work experience that includes management positions and leadership. They do not immediately reject applicants who are undergraduates as long as the student has demonstrated leadership potential in summer employment or internships. Still, the readers prefer applicants who have at least a few years of work experience. If the candidate clearly has not met the academic standards of the program and demonstrated the potential for leadership in business, she is rejected at this stage.

The second reading is conducted by an admissions office staff member. He or she looks at much the same criteria as did the first reader. The second reader pays particularly close attention to the written material in the application—the cover letter, resume, and essays. He or she is looking for the personal characteristics and professional background that indicate that the candidate will benefit from an M.B.A program as well as contribute to it. If the second reader has any doubts, she will ask a third reader to examine the application.

If the second reader thinks the candidate has potential, she will call the applicant in for an interview. During the interview, the staff member is looking for confirmation of what they have read in the application: the degree of professionalism, the ability to communicate, and the way the applicant presents herself. In addition, the interviewer may question the applicant about specific aspects of the application.

When the admissions committee finally meets to make its decision, the person who has done the interview presents the candidate to the entire committee, describing strengths and weaknesses. You can see that in this system, the interview is extremely important because the interviewer becomes the applicant's advocate. On the basis of this presentation and the discussion that follows, the committee votes on each applicant.

ELEMENTS OF AN APPLICATION

From our description of the various admissions committees, you can see that you cannot always tell which parts of your application will be considered most important by a particular admissions committee. For that reason, you should work hard to make each element of your application the best it can possibly be. For each program to which you apply, you will have to submit a number of items to make your application complete. For most programs, these include:

- An application form
- Undergraduate and other transcripts
- Graduate admissions test scores
- Letters of recommendation
- Personal essay(s)
- Tape, portfolio, writing sample, or audition for fine arts and design applicants
- The application fee

For tips on writing the personal essay, see Chapter 7.

In addition, a personal interview may be required for some programs, although for most an interview is optional. Be sure you read the information packet thoroughly so you understand what each program expects of you. They may require additional items, such as a resume.

The basic elements of an application, except the personal essay, are discussed below. Since the personal essay is such an important—and difficult—item to compose, we've devoted a whole chapter to tips on writing it (see Chapter 7).

The Application Form

On the application form, you provide basic information, such as the program or department to which you are applying; your name, social security number, address, and contact information; your citizenship status; your demographic background (usually optional); your current employer and position; your educational background; names of people who are providing references (ask them first!); and admissions test dates. Sometimes, the application form also includes a section for applying for financial aid. A separate application form for financial aid may be necessary. Be sure you understand what forms you need to submit and to whom if you are applying for aid.

If possible, you should type the information on the application form or fill out the form on line at the program's Web site. If neither option is available, print your entries neatly. Be sure you do not accidentally omit information and double-check to make sure there are no spelling errors. Remember that you will be competing against people whose forms are complete, legible, and error free.

"Take your time filling out all the necessary information, no matter how tedious it may be," advises Tammy Hammershoy, who is earning a master's degree in English at Western Connecticut State University. "Read everything very carefully, and follow all instructions. If you really want to get into the program of your choice, be patient and careful when filling out application forms and other materials." Some of the tedium may be relieved if you are applying to professional schools and can use one of the national application services, which are described later in the chapter.

Transcripts

As proof of your academic background, you will need to submit official transcripts from each college and university you have attended, even if you have taken just one course from that institution. To request official transcripts, contact the registrars of your undergraduate college and other institutions you have attended. Be sure to allow two or three months for your request to be processed. It will save time if you call ahead to find out what the fee for each transcript is and what information they need in order to pull your file and send the transcript to the proper recipient. Then you can enclose a check for that amount with your written request.

When you review your transcript, look for weaknesses that may need explanations. For example, a low GPA one semester, a very poor grade in a course, or even a below-average overall GPA may hurt your chances of acceptance unless you have good reasons for them. You can explain any shortfalls in your transcripts in your personal essay, cover letter, or addendum to the application (see Chapter 7).

If you have been out of school for years and have been successful in your professional and postgraduate endeavors, do not assume that a poor undergraduate GPA will not count against you because it's ancient history. For example, one 58-year-old prospective graduate student who had an A– average in his previous master's program but a C average as an undergraduate found that the A– did not cancel out the C. He had to take a semester of master's-level courses and achieve a minimum B average before he was admitted to the new master's program as a matriculating student.

Standardized Test Scores

Like your GPA, your admissions test scores are numbers that pop right out of your application and tell the admissions committee something about you before they have even begun reading your file. Your scores give the admissions committee a way to compare your performance to that of every other applicant to the program, even though you all may have attended very different colleges with very different instructional and grading standards.

Although your GRE scores may not be directly relevant to the field in which you are planning to work, such as one of the sciences, the scores do predict how well you can cope with the types of tasks graduate students face all the time—reading, analytical thinking, and writing. "Over the years, we have found that students with poor verbal scores do not have the ability to read and write at the graduate level," says Gail Ashley, Professor of Geological Sciences at Rutgers University in New Jersey. Still, it is rare for an admissions committee to reject an applicant solely on the basis of poor test scores. "We have no statistical cutoff," says Thomas Rochon, dean of the School of Politics and Economics at Claremont Graduate University in California, referring to both GRE scores and GPA. "But low scores mean that the admissions committee may just look through the application very quickly." Or, the admissions committee may scrutinize an application with low scores even more thoroughly to see if other qualifications compensate for poor test performance.

You should plan on taking the graduate admissions test about a year before you plan to enroll—earlier if you are taking the MCAT.

This will give you plenty of time for score reports to be submitted and plenty of time to retake the test if your first set of scores is lower than you had hoped. When you register for a graduate admissions test, you can request that the testing service send your official scores to the institutions you designate on the registration form. If you later decide to apply to additional programs and need more score reports, you can then request these in writing. Needless to say, there is a fee for each score report.

Letters of Recommendation

You will have to provide letters of recommendation for each program to which you apply. These letters are important because, like the personal essay, they give the members of the admissions committee a more personal view of you than is possible from your grades and test scores. Good letters of recommendation can tremendously increase your chances of admission and funding and lukewarm letters can harm your application. So it's important to approach the task of choosing and preparing your letter writers in a thoughtful and timely fashion.

In fact, it's a good idea to start asking for references at least six months before your application deadline. "Contact the people who will be writing letters of recommendation well in advance of application deadlines," suggests Felecia Bartow, an M.S.W. candidate at Washington University in St. Louis. "Many professionals and academics are extremely busy, and the more time that you can give them to work on your recommendation, the more it will reflect who you are." Starting early will also give you an opportunity to follow up with those who recommend you before the application deadlines.

Most of your letters of recommendation should be written by faculty members.

Choosing People to Write Recommendations

Most of your recommendations should be from faculty members, because (1) they are in the best position to judge you as a potential graduate student and (2) members of the admissions committee will consider them peers and will be more inclined to trust their judgment of you. Having professors write your letters is absolutely essential if you are applying to academic programs.

If you cannot make up the full complement of letters from faculty members or if you are applying to professional programs, you can ask employers or people who know you in a professional capacity to write references for you. In fact, if you are applying to professional programs, having letters of recommendation from those already practicing in the field is a plus. But try to find people who have a relationship with the field you are entering. It won't do you much good to have a glowing letter of recommendation from your manager at the insurance company if you are applying to a program in history or social work.

When you are trying to decide whom to ask for recommendations, keep these criteria in mind. The people you ask should:

- have a high opinion of you
- know you well, preferably in more than one context
- be familiar with your field
- be familiar with the programs to which you are applying
- have taught a large number of students (or have managed a large number of employees) so they have a good basis upon which to compare you (favorably!) to your peers
- be recognized by the admissions committee as someone whose opinion can be trusted
- have good writing skills
- be reliable enough to write and mail the letter on time

A tall order? Yes. It's likely that no one person you choose will meet all of these criteria, but try to find people who come close to this ideal.

"The most important thing to remember is that you want the writers of these letters to be very familiar with you and your work," advises Cindy Liutkus. "As I was choosing professors to ask for letters, many people gave me advice as to who would write the best letter. Some suggested that the chair of the department carries the most weight, even if he or she doesn't know you very well. Others said to ask the dean of the school, but once again, since he didn't know me very well, I was skeptical as to the quality of the letter. Instead, I chose a professor from each of my major disciplines, namely my thesis adviser and my favorite undergraduate geology professor. I needed a third, and had a lot of trouble deciding whom to ask. I eventually chose the woman in the geology department whom I respected the most....Although I had only one class with her, I felt she would give the most honest and straight-forward account of my undergraduate accomplishments, my personality and work habits, and my goals for the future."

Approaching Your Letter Writers

Once you've decided whom you plan to ask for references, be diplomatic. Don't simply show up in their offices, ask them to write a letter, and give them the recommendation forms. Plan your approach so that you leave the potential recommendation writer, as well as yourself, a graceful "out" in case one reacts less than enthusiastically.

On your first approach, you should remind the potential recommendation writers about who you are (if necessary) and then ask whether they think they can write you a good letter of recommendation. This gives them a chance to say no. If they agree but hesitate or seem to be less than enthusiastic, you can thank them for agreeing to help you. Later, you can write them a note saying that you won't need a letter of recommendation after all. On the other hand, if any of them seem genuinely pleased to help you, you can then make an appointment to give them the recommendation forms and the other information they will need.

A confidential letter usually has more validity in the eyes of the admissions committee.

Waiving Your Right to See a Letter

The recommendation forms in your application packets contain a waiver. If you sign the waiver, you give up your right to see the letter of recommendation. Before you decide to sign it, discuss the waiver with each person who is writing you a reference. Some people will write you a reference only if you agree to sign the waiver and they can be sure the letter is confidential. This does not necessarily mean they intend to write a negative letter; instead, it means that they think a confidential letter will carry more weight with the admissions committee. In fact, they are right. A confidential letter usually has more validity in the eyes of the admissions committee. From the committee's point of view, an open letter may be less than candid because the letter writer knows you will read it. In general, it's better to waive your right to see a letter. If this makes you anxious in regard to a particular recommendation writer, do not choose that person to write a letter.

Helping Your Letter Writers

Once a faculty member or employer has agreed to write a letter of recommendation for you, they will wants to write something positive on your behalf. No matter how great you are, this won't be possible if the letter writer cannot remember you and your accomplishments very well. "Help faculty members write a more effective letter by reminding them of what you've done," advises Teresa Shaw, Associate Dean for Arts and Humanities at Claremont Graduate University in California. "Letters that are not specific are ineffective letters."

When you meet with your letter writers to give them the forms, use the opportunity to provide them with information about yourself. Bring a short resume that highlights your academic, professional, and personal accomplishments. List the course(s) you took with them, the grades you received, and any significant work you did, such as a big research paper or lab project. The resume can be the basis of a conversation with the letter writer, amplifying your notable accomplishments. "Many of the people I asked to write me recommendation letters found it helpful if I wrote down a list of my accomplishments and my plans," recalls Jenn Wagaman, a master's candidate in public communications at the University of Alaska at Fairbanks. "Even though these people knew me, they wrote better letters because they had the exact information right in front of them."

What should you do if the letter writer asks you to draft the letter? Accept gracefully. Then pretend you are the writer and craft a letter extolling your virtues and accomplishments in detail. Remember, if the letter writer does not like what you've written, he is free to change it in the final draft.

You can help your letter writers by filling in as much of the information as you can on the letter of recommendation forms. It's also a nice gesture to provide stamped, addressed envelopes for the letters if they are to be mailed directly to the programs or to you for inclusion in your application. Be sure your letter writers understand what their deadlines are. In other words, do everything you can to expedite the process, especially since you may be approaching your professors at the beginning of the fall semester, when they are the busiest.

Finally, send thank you notes to professors and employers who have come through for you with letters of recommendation. Remember that you are hoping someday to be their colleague in academia or a profession. Cementing good relationships now can help you in the future.

Using the Placement Office

Most college placement offices will handle letters of recommendation on behalf of students. The office establishes a file for each student using this service, and they place a copy of the letter of recommendation from each professor in the student's file. When you are ready, request that the placement office send a copy of each letter to each program to which you are applying. This service is convenient for professors because it relieves them of the responsibility of sending out multiple copies. On the down side, letters written for a placement office file often have a generic, "one size fits all" approach. You may be better off begging your professors to write individual letters that are specific to the programs to which you are applying to.

If you are an undergraduate and unsure of your plans for graduate school, you can ask your professors to write you letters of recommendation now, when you are still fresh in their minds. Have the letters placed in your file in the placement office and ask the office to keep your file active. Although there may be a fee for this service, it's worth it. When you do apply to graduate school a few years down the road, you will already have several letters of recommendation that you can use.

If You've Been Out of School for Years

What should you do if you have been out of school for years and have lost touch with your professors? If you established a file of letters of recommendation at the placement office when you were an undergraduate, you will now reap the benefit of your foresight. But if you did not, there are several things you can do to overcome the problems associated with the passage of time.

First, if a professor is still teaching at your alma mater, you can get in touch by mail or e-mail, reminding the person who you are, what you've done since they taught you, your plans for graduate school, and a resume. Tell the professor what you remember most about their courses. Most professors keep their course records for at least a few years and can look up your grades. If you are still near your undergraduate institution, you can make your request in person. "I arranged to meet one of my college professors for coffee to talk about what I had been doing in the five years since she had me as a student," says Felecia Bartow. "It gave me a chance to bring her up to date on my experience, and it gave her a lot more information with which to write her recommendation." Once you've made this initial approach, you can then call and ask whether the professor thinks they can write a strong recommendation for you.

Another strategy if you've been out of school for a while is to obtain letters of recommendation from faculty members teaching in the programs to which you plan to apply. In order to obtain such a letter, you may have to take a course in the program before you enroll so that the faculty member gets to know you. Members of an admissions committee will hesitate to reject a candidate who has been strongly recommended by one of their colleagues.

Finally, if you are having trouble recruiting professors to recommend you, call the programs to which you are applying and ask what their policy is for applicants in your situation. They may waive the letters of recommendation, allow you to substitute letters from employers, or ask you to take relevant courses at a nearby institution in order to obtain letters from faculty members. Remember, if you are applying to an academic rather than a professional program, letters from employers will not carry as much weight with the admissions committee as letters from faculty members. In fact, many academics are not at all impressed by work experience because they feel it does not predict how successful you will be as a graduate student.

Portfolios, Writing Samples, Tapes, and Auditions

If you are applying to programs in the fine arts, design, or architecture, you will be required to demonstrate your artistic or design abilities by means of a portfolio, writing sample, videotape, audiotape, or audition. Students in the visual arts must present a portfolio of their work, usually in slide format, so that admissions committee members can judge their talent, conceptual ability, level of competence, and technical skill. Film students may have to submit a film on which they have worked. Students applying to an M.F.A. program in writing will generally have to submit a sample of their written work. If you are an undergraduate or recent college graduate, take the opportunity to work with a professor in compiling your submission. Your professor will have a good idea of what will impress an admissions committee.

Most music and performing arts students must audition as part of the application process. In fact, the more selective the institution, the more important and brief the audition generally is. At the most competitive schools, an audition may last only 5 to 10 minutes. Although some schools hold regional auditions in different cities, in most cases you are expected to travel to the school. If travel would be a hardship, some schools may permit you to send a tape of your performance in lieu of an audition. Still, if you can audition in person, you should do so. In addition to giving the faculty members an opportunity to judge your abilities, an audition gives you the opportunity to evaluate a school first-hand. Since the requirements and instructions for auditions and tapes vary considerably, be sure you understand what each program expects of you in order to prepare properly for your auditions.

Interviews

A graduate school interview is similar to a job interview— dress accordingly.

Interviews are usually required by medical schools and are sometimes required by business schools and other programs. But in most cases an interview is not necessary. However, if you think you do well in interviews, you can call each program and request an interview. "I made sure I got an opportunity to interview with admissions staff," recalls Naaz Qureshi, an M.B.A. candidate at the Cox School of Business at Southern Methodist University, "since interviewing has always been my strong suit." A good interview may be an opportunity to sway the admissions committee in your favor. Human nature being what it is, an excellent half-hour interview may loom larger in the minds of admissions staff and faculty members than four years of average grades.

Most interviewers are interested in the way you approach problems, think, and articulate your ideas, and so they will concentrate on questions that will reveal these aspects of your character, not on questions that test your technical knowledge. They may ask you controversial questions or give you hypothetical problems to solve. Or they may ask about your professional goals, motivation for graduate study, and areas of interest—much the same material that is in your personal essay. Remember that interviewers are interested more in how you think than in *what* you think.

When you prepare for an interview, it would be helpful if you have already written your personal essay, because the thought processes involved in preparing the essay will help you articulate many of the issues that are likely to come up in an interview. It is also helpful to do your homework on the program, so if the opportunity arises for you to ask questions, you can do so intelligently. Finally, be sure you are dressed properly. That means dressing as if you are going to a professional job interview.

Fees

Each application must be accompanied by a fee, or your papers are likely to sit in the admissions office without action. If you cannot afford the fee, you can ask the admissions office and your undergraduate financial aid office for a fee waiver.

If you are applying to half a dozen schools, you can see that the costs will mount quickly. In addition to the program application fees, you must pay transcript fees, test fees, score report fees, photocopying fees, mailing costs, and travel costs if you are interviewing or auditioning. "Put aside some money for the process—it will cost more than you expect, especially if you are interviewing," suggests Jennifer Cheavens, a Ph.D. candidate in clinical psychology at the University of Kansas at Lawrence. The application process may cost hundreds of dollars, even more if you are applying to many schools.

SUBMITTING YOUR APPLICATION

As we mentioned at the beginning of the chapter, you should submit your completed applications well before they are due. *Be sure to keep a copy of everything.* You can either mail the application to the admissions offices, or you can file portions of it on line through the programs' Web sites. Remember, however, that some elements of the application, such as the fee and official transcripts, will still need to be mailed in paper form. Also note that most schools that accept online applications simply print them and process them as if they had come in by regular mail.

Try to submit all of your materials at once; this simplifies the task of compiling and tracking your application at the admissions office. If that's impossible, as it is for many students, keep track of missing items and forward them as soon as possible. Remember that if items are missing, your application is likely to sit in the admissions office. According to Suzette Vandeburg at the State University of New York at Binghamton, incomplete applications are held for a year and then they are tossed.

Using National Application Services

In a few professional fields, such as business, law, medicine, osteopathy, dentistry, and podiatry, there are national services that coordinate part of the application process for member institutions. You send your data to the service, where it is processed and forwarded to the schools to which you are applying. The admissions offices of the professional schools then add other elements of your application, such as letters of recommendation, to the standardized data. You can find out whether there is a national service in your field of interest from your adviser or a school in which you are interested.

GradAdvantage for Graduate and Business Schools

GradAdvantage is a new application service developed by the Educational Testing Service and Peterson's. GradAdvantage can save you a lot of time and work by allowing you to apply on line to many graduate schools and M.B.A. programs. You enter your personal data, educational background, employment history, and activities only once, and this information is automatically posted to the application forms of the schools you select. You can then complete each application online at your convenience, saving your work in progress whenever you've finished a session. You can write your essays using your own word processor and then upload them into your online applications. And you can submit the names of the people who will be writing your letters of recommendation.

GradAdvantage sends your application and your GRE, GMAT and TOEFL scores (if applicable) via the Internet to the admissions office of the schools you have designated. For more information, check the GradAdvantage Web site at http://www.gradadvantage.org.

Law School Data Assembly Services

The Law School Admissions Council, which administers the LSAT, provides the Law School Data Assembly Services (LSDAS), also called Law Services, to handle applications to member schools. When you register for the LSAT you can also subscribe to LSDAS for an additional fee, or you can subscribe to the service at a later date. You provide Law Services with personal information along with information on every college, graduate, or professional school you have ever attended, including dates of attendance, area of concentration, and degrees awarded or expected. In addition, you will request that an official transcript from each of these schools be sent to Law Services. When Law Services receives your LSAT scores, personal and educational information, and official transcripts, it prepares a report and sends you a copy. Needless to say, you should check the report carefully and have any errors corrected. The law schools to which you apply may then request a copy of your report directly from Law Services. You are responsible for submitting the other elements of your application, including the specific application form, essays, and letters of recommendation, directly to each law school.

American Medical Colleges Application Service

The Association of American Medical Colleges runs a service similar to the LSDAS. If you are applying to medical schools, you send your complete application with essay and transcripts to the American Medical Colleges Application Service (AMCAS). AMCAS sends copies of your application materials to the medical schools you have designated. With this service, your application is standardized, and your essay cannot be tailored to any particular school.

However, not all medical schools use AMCAS. If you are applying to any of those schools, you will have to submit individual applications according to each school's instructions. The MCAT booklet lists schools that use the AMCAS and schools that do not.

Following Up

It's important that you check on the status of your applications, especially if you don't receive acknowledgment that an application is complete. Give the admissions office a couple of weeks to process your application and then call to find out if it's complete. Usually the missing items are transcripts or letters of recommendation. "Don't assume," warns Rose Ann Trantham, Assistant Director of Graduate Admissions and Records for the University of Tennessee at Knoxville. "Follow up—not every week, but call periodically." Suzette Vandeburg of the State University of New York at Binghamton agrees; she advises applicants to be proactive about their applications. "Check in periodically," says Vandeburg. "E-mail is a great way to check on your application."

Cindy Liutkus remembers how anxious she was about her applications. "The application process is definitely nerve-wracking," Liutkus says. "I was always worried that something wouldn't make it on time. I eventually sent stamped postcards along with every application and asked that the department secretary check the package and send the card along if everything was okay." Not content with that, Liutkus made sure by following up with e-mail, too.

> **It's important that you check the status of your applications, especially if you don't receive acknowledgment that an application is complete.**

IN SUMMARY

Preparing a thorough, focused, and well-written application is one of the most important tasks you will ever undertake. In addition to gaining you admission to a graduate program that can help you achieve your goals, a good application may win you enough monetary support to finance your degree. With these future benefits in mind, work on your applications as if they are the most important things you can possibly be doing—because they are.

Writing a Good Personal Essay

The application to graduate school is not all numbers and outside evaluations. Admissions committees are also interested in finding out about you as an individual and in more intangible qualities, like your ability to write a good essay. Thus the personal essay is the part of the application in which you can take control and demonstrate who you are and why you deserve to be admitted. Other parts of your application—test scores, GPA, and undergraduate transcripts—may reflect your academic ability but not much else. The letters of recommendation are beyond your control once you've chosen the writers. But a good personal essay can make you stand out from other applicants. It can show the committee the qualities that will make you an excellent graduate student and professional. In other words, the essay is your showcase and you should make the most of it. Even if you can write superb prose in your sleep, you still need to know what to write. In this chapter, you'll get a step-by-step guide to preparing the personal essay.

WHAT THE ADMISSIONS COMMITTEE LOOKS FOR

When they read an essay, the members of an admissions committee look for evidence that you are prepared for graduate school, have demonstrated intellectual or professional growth, and are focused and interested in a particular field. They want to know what you hope to get out of your graduate education. They are not particularly interested in your personal, psychological development. Autobiographical details and feelings, unless they help explain your intellectual and professional interests, are not relevant to an admissions committee. Instead, they want to know whether you will make a good student and colleague.

The admissions committee gleans most of this information from what you write. But they can also tell a lot from how you write. If your writing is clear and conveys your ideas effectively, you are demonstrating your ability to communicate. If your writing is free of grammatical and spelling errors, you are demonstrating your attention to detail. Good writing skills are essential for a graduate student in any field, so a poorly written essay can hurt an application. A well-written statement, on the other hand, will help your case.

Requirements Vary from Field to Field

The essays required of graduate applicants vary widely. For some programs, you may just have to explain in one or two paragraphs why you want to go to graduate school. In the sciences and engineering, for example, the essay may simply be a means of conveying information about your research experience and interests. "I don't think my essay was all that remarkable," recalls a Ph.D. candidate in physics at Harvard University. "Grad schools in science look for a clear-minded view on the student's part as to their research plans." J. W. Viers, Director of Graduate Studies for the chemistry department at Virginia Tech, explains, "The personal essay doesn't carry much weight. We are simply looking for an indication that the applicant has done research and enjoys doing research."

In contrast, the business schools pay a lot of attention to the personal essay because your professional experience is an important criterion for admission. In fact, a business school application may call for two, three, or even more essays on different topics such as:

- Why do you want to pursue an M.B.A.?
- Describe one of your passions.
- If an article were to be written about you ten years from now, what would it say?
- Describe an experience you had as a member of a team in a professional capacity.
- What is your most memorable work experience?
- Describe a failure and how you dealt with it.

Donna Lau Smith, Director of M.B.A. Admissions for Cox School of
Business, Southern Methodist University, says that the essays are
meant to give the admissions committee a good sense of who a person
is. "The drive, commitment, and initiative needed to do well in business
school is a part of personality, and it's not necessarily shown in GMAT
scores or GPA," explains Smith. "That's why it's critical to provide
good written materials." Adds Janelle Heineke, Associate Dean for
Graduate Programs at Boston University's School of Management,
"The essays help us judge the work and life experiences that an
applicant brings to the program."

For applicants in literature or the arts, the personal essay may be
judged on its creativity or style as well as the information it conveys.
Melany Kahn, who has an M.F.A. in film from New York University,
recalls that she tried to be imaginative when writing her essay. "At
NYU, it's imperative to show imagination and the ability to tell a story,
not all your technical experience." Megan McAfee, an M.F.A. candidate
in costume technology at Virginia Tech, says, "I think my essay was
really unusual since I wasn't going to go to a place that didn't like me
and I wasn't going to puff myself up to be something I'm not. But I
think that's probably an attitude that someone in theater can take."

A Word about Creativity

A word of warning about creativity. It's fine to be creative within the
confines of the genre. But admissions committees usually look askance
at essays that are too creative. The law school applicant who wrote her
essay in the form of LSAT questions undermined her application, as did
the English literature applicant whose essay was written in light verse.
Resist the temptation to be clever or cute; it's likely to backfire.

**Resist the
temptation to be
clever or cute; it's
likely to backfire.**

THINK BEFORE YOU WRITE

Do you remember the self-assessment you did in Chapter 2? You
answered many difficult questions about your goals, interests, strengths,
and weaknesses in order to decide whether graduate school was right
for you. If you did an honest and thorough job of assessing yourself, you

will have already thought through many of the issues you will need to address when writing your personal essay.

Things to Think About

Your self-assessment should make it easier for you to get a handle on issues such as:

- how you came to be interested in a field and why you think you are well suited to it
- aspects of your life that make you uniquely qualified to pursue study in a field
- experiences or qualities that distinguish you from other applicants
- unusual hardships or obstacles that you've had to overcome
- unusual accomplishments, whether personal, professional, or academic
- professional experiences that have contributed to your personal growth
- how your skills and personal characteristics would contribute to success in this field
- your personal and professional goals and their relationship to graduate education

In addition, when you researched and evaluated programs to which you would apply, you learned a lot about the programs that were good matches for you. In your essay, you will also have to address issues like:

- what appeals to you about a particular program
- how your interests and strengths match the needs of the program

Use the Writing Process to Clarify Your Thoughts

Needless to say, this type of introspection is difficult and articulating its results can be even harder. Brenda Bennett, who earned a master's degree in special education from Cambridge College in Massachusetts, recalls, "[The personal essay] forced me to evaluate my own belief system and philosophy of education. How different I am today than only seven years ago when I started in this field. It was a real eye-opening experience."

Leslie Nelman, a Master of Arts candidate in translation and interpretation at the Monterey Institute of International Studies in California, struggled to clarify her background and goals. "The 'Statement of Purpose' was supposed to include 'educational and career objectives' and describe how I acquired my language proficiency. All of this in 600 words or less. Once you get started, 600 words isn't really that long! It is difficult articulating exactly what it is you want to do with the rest of your life, whether you're 52 (as I was) or 22. It took several false starts and about three days to put it together."

Be yourself. Don't try to second-guess what the committee is looking for. They can tell.

BE YOURSELF...

The most common words of advice from most admissions directors about writing the personal essay are to be yourself. Remember, you are seeking to be accepted by a program that is a good match for you. If you disguise who you really are in an effort to impress an admissions committee, you are doing yourself—and them—a disservice. "Be who you are. Don't try to second-guess what the committee is looking for," Donna Lau Smith advises. "We can tell."

Cindy Liutkus, a Ph.D. candidate in geology at Rutgers, struggled with her essay for several weeks. "Eventually, though, I just wrote my thoughts and feelings....I think grad schools read an essay that's written from the heart and they realize that the student is passionate about their work, dedicated to their future in that field, and comfortable with expressing themselves."

In this introduction, Liutkus is candid about the late flowering of her interest in geology. She does not sidestep the problems that arose because of the late declaration of her major. In other words, she is straightforward and honest about her interest in geology and the shortcomings in her preparation. This essay helped Liutkus gain admission to several programs in geology.

Here is the beginning of Liutkus's essay:

> The decision to further my education in the area of geological sciences came later in my college career than for many others. I was originally a philosophy major

with only a minor in geology, even though it is an area of study which has fascinated me since I was a child.... However, as I continued to take more advanced classes in the field, I became more convinced that a major in geology would better represent my true interests.

It was during my junior year abroad, while studying in Melbourne, Australia, that the decision to double major in both philosophy and geology became final. However, with such a late decision, I was caught between a rock and a hard place. I had made the decision to follow my true interest but now had to play catch-up with the other students in the field in order to fulfill the requirements of the major. Despite doubling up on lab sciences during my senior year, I still have some gaps in the areas of calculus, chemistry, and physics. However, I plan to complete these classes upon enrollment in a graduate program.

So, be honest. If you demonstrate self-knowledge by presenting your strengths as well as your limitations, your essay will be a true reflection of who you are.

...BUT BE DIPLOMATIC

Honesty is important, but so is diplomacy. Try not to reveal weaknesses in your personality, such as laziness, dishonesty, or selfishness. Don't say you want to attend a program because it's cheap, within commuting distance, or you know you can get in. Even though these things may be true, they are not reasons with which the admissions committee will be sympathetic. Instead, frame your points in a positive light: you can fulfill its admission requirements because you have the proper prerequisites; you live nearby and know of its reputation; and so on.

WRITE A STRONG OPENING

When you write your essay, put yourself in the position of an admissions committee member who may read fifty or a hundred essays in a day or two. By the end of all this reading, the poor individual may be bored to tears and would be pleased by any essay that simply engages his or her interest. How are you going to accomplish this? By writing an opening that grabs the reader's attention.

Describe an Important Experience

"Many essays begin, 'I would like to go to graduate school because...,'" complains Gladys Fleckles, Director of Graduate Studies at California State University in Fullerton. "This is boring! Instead, describe a pivotal experience that made you decide that graduate school is what you want to do." Nestor Montilla, who is pursuing a master's degree in public administration at John Jay College of Criminal Justice in New York, described an experience that strengthened his desire to go to graduate school.

> My foremost reason [for pursuing graduate education] is my passion for public service....My aspiration was partially fulfilled after Ruth Messinger, Manhattan Borough President, appointed me as a member of Planning Board 12. Thanks to this opportunity, my commitment to public service has reinforced my quest for civic responsibility. Indeed, the spirit of helping our community to be a better place to live is what inspires me to pursue graduate studies.

By mentioning his planning board appointment, Montilla shows that he has a real interest in and experience with public service, both of which are solid reasons for pursuing a degree in public administration. "Look deep within yourself for something profound that has happened to you," advises Naaz Qureshi, an M.B.A. candidate at Cox School of Business, Southern Methodist University. "Admissions officers look for defining moments in a person's life that forever changed them."

The opening is also the place to set forth any unusual experience you have had that has contributed significantly to the person you are today. The experience may be growing up poor, being an Olympic athlete, or moving to the United States at the age of 14. Whatever the experience is, show how it has formed your character and life and how it relates to the graduate education you now want to pursue.

Be Specific

What if you have not had a defining moment or experience that sparked your interest in graduate studies? Then write an opening that is specific enough to have some real interest. Here is the first paragraph from Leslie Nelman's statement of purpose.

> In applying for admission to the translation and interpretation program at Monterey Institute of International Studies, I'm following through on a goal I set for myself over thirty years ago. I have always been fascinated by language, first by my mother tongue, then by other languages, once I became aware of their existence. The 'cold war' that was raging when I was young was a war of words. It occurred to me then that misunderstandings were likely when everything had to be translated for the international policy makers. Surely translators and interpreters played a key role in the fate of nations! And so my fascination with language grew into a vague career goal.

In this paragraph, Nelman describes the development of her interest in language and her realization of the importance that language plays in international affairs. The paragraph is specific enough to engage the reader's interest and make him or her want to continue. The key is to remember that specific details are usually more interesting than general statements. Be specific and you'll have a better chance of connecting with your readers.

TELL HOW YOUR STORY INTERSECTS WITH THEIRS

If you are applying to several programs, you will be tempted to write a boilerplate essay. Resist the temptation. Admissions committees grow adept at picking out the generic personal statements. "It always shows if it's a boilerplate statement," says Teresa Shaw, Associate Dean for the Arts and Humanities at Claremont Graduate University in California. "The personal statement should be written to the particular school. It's impressive if a student shows he knows the program, its research areas, and its professors."

Describe Why You Are a Match for Them

Remember that when you were evaluating programs, you were looking for a good match for you. The personal essay is the place where you can explain to the admissions committee why you are a good match for them. According to Gladys Fleckles, "The key question is: Why should you be selected over anyone else? Tell about your skills and interest in the program. Be specific. Why would you be an asset to their program?" The story of your intellectual and professional development and your goals should culminate in your reasons for choosing this particular program. Your reasons should reflect a knowledge of the program's faculty members, key research areas, and other characteristics.

Jennifer Cheavens, a Ph.D. candidate in clinical psychology at the University of Kansas at Lawrence, wrote a different version of her essay for each program to which she applied. "I... found that tailoring the autobiographical statement to the different schools that I was applying to was helpful in helping me really decide that I matched with a program," says Cheavens. "I tried to make the personal statement specific to each program for two reasons. One, so they would know I was really interested and had done my homework. Two, so I was sure that was somewhere I could be for five years."

In the following paragraphs of her essay, Cathy Chappell, who earned a master's degree in educational foundations at the University of Cincinnati, explains why she wants to continue in its doctoral program.

> I continue to be attracted to the interdisciplinary aspect of the Educational Foundations Graduate Program. I appreciate the broad range of perspectives in the study of education and feel particularly drawn to the sociology and anthropology disciplines. The Education Foundations Department is concerned with the problems of urban education and I find the emphasis on group

dynamics and interaction to have great functional value. An examination of the patterns of subordination and domination of groups in society, although occurring in every institutional setting, reveals disparities in equality that are profound and salient in the urban educational setting. Dominant groups structure these institutions to maintain their dominance and subordinate groups must struggle for equality...

I find the prospect of continued study in the Educational Foundations program very exciting and am impressed with the department's professors and their progressive, interactive scholarship. If accepted into the Doctoral Program, I plan to expand my knowledge base, to increase and hone my research and writing abilities, and to contribute significant analysis to the study, understanding, and amelioration of structural and individual causes of educational disparities. I appreciate the opportunity to extend my study to include other departments within the College and University and I look forward to expanding my limited teaching experience. My ultimate goals, as of yet undecided, include research within school systems and communities and a possible position in higher education. I feel that my background and aspirations fit well within the philosophies and goals of the Department of Educational Foundations. I am eager and prepared to continue as a dedicated and enthusiastic member of the graduate student body of the Department.

Use the Catalog as a Resource

Although Chappell had the benefit of being familiar with the doctoral program because she was a master's student, you can use the knowledge you've gained from researching the program if you don't know it first-hand. In particular, the program catalog can be a good resource when you are writing this section of the essay. "I read the Simmons

College School of Library and Information Science's catalog thoroughly several times before deciding to apply. The time was well spent," recalls a master's candidate in library and information science. "It is important to know what specific programs, services, faculty member expertise, and resources a grad school has to offer before writing the essay. The admissions committee will be looking for a good fit for their program."

In his personal statement, Bob Connelly, who earned an Ed.D. in educational administration from Seton Hall University in New Jersey, explains why he would be an asset to a cohort-based executive degree program in which students, who are all educational administrators, enter as a group and stay together during the time it takes to earn the degree.

> Now that I have made the decision to commit to the program, I need to balance optimism with the realities of meeting success in the program. I will outline personal qualities that are predictors of success. I believe that I possess the intellect, pragmatism, discipline, drive, and determination as well as the interpersonal skills to be a success in this doctoral program. I define success as completing the program within the prescribed time and contributing to the professional growth and development not only of myself but of the entire cohort that will be venturing through this exciting new program planned by Seton Hall.

In this paragraph, Connelly explains why he is a good match for the Seton Hall program's instructional design. In this case, being a good match involves more than academic considerations. It involves the self-discipline to keep up with a paced program and the interpersonal skills to contribute to the educational experience of the cohort.

In addition to identifying the tangible characteristics of a program, you can also get a sense of its philosophy and values from the catalog. "Go through the school catalog and look for certain attributes that the school values and try and incorporate them into your essays," suggests Naaz Qureshi.

DESCRIBE YOUR GOALS

In most essays, you will have to explain how a graduate degree will help you achieve your goals. Even if you are not sure exactly what you want to do professionally, describe what you might be interested in doing once you receive the degree. Indicating that you have a purpose in obtaining a graduate degree shows that you are focused and motivated and have a real sense of the possibilities.

Nestor Montilla's objective in pursuing a master's degree in public administration was to enable him to do meaningful work in the public sector. Here is how he explained his aspirations in his personal essay.

> Having a clear sense of what I want to be, I planned ahead and enrolled at John Jay College [as an undergraduate] to prepare myself academically with a public service career in mind. My...goal is to acquire the political skills and the academic credentials to explore career opportunities at the managerial and teaching levels in our government agencies. I aim to become a more productive, competent professional to help in both the rebuilding of our decaying communities and in the development of more feasible and effective means to better manage our public institutions.
>
> Undoubtedly, an advanced degree will help me to accomplish my plans, as the above considerations indicate. Then, after exploring career opportunities in the public sector, I will be professionally ready to pursue a doctoral or law degree as part of my ultimate career objectives.

Notice that Montilla indicates both a short-term goal and possible long-term goals that his degree would help him achieve. Cindy Liutkus's goal is long-term—to earn a Ph.D. in order to teach at the university level and continue to do field work. She explains what she hopes to accomplish with graduate study.

> Through my graduate study, I intend to expand my knowledge of geology while focusing on and conducting research in the areas of sedimentology and stratigraphy. In addition to my interest in these areas, my teaching assistantships and tutor position have been extremely

gratifying, especially when I am able to motivate others and help them understand. Because of this, and due in large part to the influence of my undergraduate professor, Edward Cotter, Ph.D., I have decided that my ultimate goal is to teach at the college level. Teaching, for me, provides a vehicle for stimulation and exchange of ideas, an opportunity to remain current with related literature, and an appropriate atmosphere for original research design. Furthermore, continued field work would enhance my contribution to the classroom. In short, teaching will fulfill all my personal and professional goals.

A final example is from Leslie Nelman's personal statement. In her concluding paragraph, Nelman ties together her background, her proposed studies, and her career objectives.

What I hope to do at this point in my life is integrate what I have learned in the business world with my true passion, (the German) language. I've spent the better part of this last year working intensively to refresh my language fluency and my understanding of contemporary German issues, politics, attitudes, etc. More specifically, I attended an eight-week advanced language course in Freiburg last summer, then spent two months each in Munich and Berlin, where I took individual instruction at the Goethe Institute while sharing an apartment with a single working woman. If my language skills are deemed adequate to the task, I would like to expand and fine-tune this background with the rigorous translation/interpretation training that the Monterey Institute offers. Given my personal circumstances, I do not have expectations of becoming an interpreter at the UN or the European Union; I anticipate, rather, working on a freelance basis on legal/

finance/insurance-related assignments, be it as interpreter or translator. I do look forward to finally playing a role in bridging the communication gap.

EXPLAIN SHORTCOMINGS IN YOUR BACKGROUND

There is a difference of opinion on whether or not the personal essay is the place to explain any weaknesses in your academic or professional preparation when you are not directly asked to do so. Some people think that the essay should concentrate on a positive presentation of your qualifications. They feel that an explanation of poor GRE scores, for example, belongs in an addendum or cover letter. Others think that the essay is the place to address your application's weaknesses. Of course, if you are applying to medical schools using AMCAS, you will not be able to attach an addendum but will have to deal with this issue in the essay.

Perhaps a good rule of thumb is to address any weaknesses or shortcomings that are directly relevant to your proposed work in your field in the essay. For example, in her essay Cindy Liutkus explained why she lacked some necessary courses to pursue a graduate degree in geology and how she planned to make them up. On the other hand, if the weak spot in your application is not directly related to your field of study, you may prefer to address it in an addendum or cover letter. For example, if like many college freshmen you had a poor GPA, you can explain this separately. Try to put a positive spin on it, too. Explain, for example, how your GPA in your major was much higher, or how your GPA improved as you matured. Essentially, your decision as to where to address your weaknesses will depend on their importance and relevance to your pursuit of a graduate degree.

DRAFTING AND EDITING

Follow the Instructions

When you sit down to draft your essay, the first thing you should make sure of is that you are *answering the question posed on the application*. Be sure you read the instructions for each program's personal statement carefully. Small differences in wording can affect how you approach writing the essay. Read these two sets of instructions for the personal statement.

1. Please state your reasons for deciding to pursue a graduate degree in the field you have chosen. Include references to your past study and research in your chosen field, your plans for study at the university, including problems and issues you want to address, and your personal goals.

2. The personal statement is an important part of your application. It is your opportunity to provide information about your background, interests and aspirations, and how they relate to your proposed academic program. In your statement, describe your reasons for pursuing graduate study, the program you hope to follow at the university, and the strengths and weaknesses of your preparation for graduate study. All personal statements should be double-spaced and typed, two to three pages.

These instructions cover more or less the same ground, but the second school asks you to describe the strengths and weaknesses of your preparation for graduate study, whereas the first school merely asks you to describe your past study. When writing the essay for the second school, therefore, you must be sure to address your preparation in greater detail. You will have to both describe and evaluate your readiness—or lack thereof.

> Don't play with font size in order to get your essay to come out the right length. Admissions officers don't really want to read eight point type.

Don't Write Too Much or Too Little

The second thing you should keep in mind as you begin your draft is the length of the essay. Often, the length is specified; for example, the second school's instructions above indicate that the statement should be two to three double-spaced pages. What should you do if length is not specified, as it is not in the first set of instructions above? Then write one to two typed pages. An essay that is shorter than one page does not allow room for you to develop your ideas. And an essay that is longer than two pages becomes a chore for the admissions committee to read.

Finally, when you write your first draft, do not waste space by repeating information that the admissions committee can get from other parts of your application, like your transcript or resume. Use the essay to provide them with new information or to highlight particular accomplishments.

Review the First Draft

Once you have drafted your essay, read the question again. Has your draft answered the question fully? If the essay is incomplete, go back and fill in the missing material. Then ask people for feedback. Although your spouse and friends may be helpful, you may get more valuable suggestions from faculty members who know you and who also know what a personal essay should be like. Ask whether you've included things you should leave out or should add things you've forgotten. Is the tone right? Have you achieved the right balance between boasting and being too modest? Are there any problems with organization, clarity, grammar, or spelling?

Felecia Bartow, an M.S.W. candidate at Washington University in St. Louis, gave her drafts to several people. "It helped to have a couple of people (from different disciplines) read various drafts of my essays in order to give me feedback on the clarity and conciseness of my writing." Jim Lipuma, a Ph.D. candidate in environmental science at the New Jersey Institute of Technology, recommends, "Proofreading goes without saying, but always read it to yourself, have someone else read it, and then read it aloud to someone. This will show all the problems, highlight the areas that need work, and allow for any weaknesses to be exposed."

When you sit down to draft your essay, the first thing you should make sure of is that you are *answering the question posed on the application*.

PREPARE THE FINAL DRAFT

Once you've revised the essay and are satisfied with your final draft, ask someone with a sharp eye to proofread it for you. The final draft should be absolutely free of grammar and spelling errors, so do not rely on grammar- or spell-checks to find all of the errors. Once you are done, be sure to keep backup files as well as a hard copy. Although you won't be able to use the whole essay for all your applications, you may be able to use parts of it. If you do work this way, be absolutely sure when you submit the final essays that you have not made any careless editing mistakes. "If you're applying to multiple schools, make sure that you don't have any 'cut and paste' errors in your application," warns Neill Kipp, a Ph.D. candidate in computer science at Virginia Tech. "If you apply to Florida State in one letter and the University of Florida in another but forget to change every occurrence of the university name, then count on being the semester-long laughingstock of the admissions office."

Finally, if you are submitting the statement on separate sheets of paper rather than on the application form itself, put your name, social security number, and the question on the essay, and type "see attached essay" on the application form.

MAKE IT YOURS

If after reading this chapter you are still daunted by the prospect of writing your personal statement, just put the whole task aside for a few days. You will find that the ideas, suggestions, and excerpts you've just read will trigger some mental activity and that soon you will have some ideas of your own to jot down.

Also remember that it's not necessary to have an exotic background or a dramatic event to recount in order to write a good essay and gain admission to a program. Admissions committees are looking for diversity—in gender, race, ethnicity, nationality, and socioeconomic status, to name some obvious characteristics. But they are also looking for people with diverse life experiences to add richness to their student body. Your background, which may seem perfectly ordinary to you, nevertheless has unique and relevant elements that can be assets to the program you choose. Your task is to identify and build upon these elements to persuade the admissions committee that you should be selected.

> **"If you apply to Florida State in one letter and the University of Florida in another but forget to change every occurrence of the university name, then count on being the semester-long laughingstock of the admissions office."**

Paying

Pursuing a master's degree or Ph.D. costs a lot of money. Pursuing a professional degree can cost even more. How are you going to pay for graduate school and support yourself at the same time? Lots of people who don't have the "work full-time, go to school part-time" option get stuck at this point when they are applying to graduate programs. Even though they have a good chance of gaining admittance to the program of their choice, they conclude that they can't afford to attend.

But that pessimistic conclusion may be unwarranted. Admittedly, finding money to help you pay for your graduate education can be difficult, in part because there are so many types and sources of funds and because information about them is scattered. Yet financial help for graduate students is available. In this chapter we'll give you an overview of the financial aid situation at the graduate level and help you get started on your search for funding.

SOME GENERAL COMMENTS ABOUT FINANCIAL AID

To give you some background for your own further investigations, we'll begin with some general information about financial aid on the graduate level. Remember, as you read these generalizations, that there are exceptions to each one. They are simply meant to provide you with an overview of what you can expect.

Merit-Based Versus Need-Based Aid

Financial aid for undergraduates is usually based on a calculation of need, but aid for graduate students is generally based on academic excellence, especially in the sciences, humanities, and arts. And excellence, for an incoming student, is judged on the basis of your application package. That's why it's so important to devote the time and effort to make all aspects of your application as good as they can be—a lot of money may depend on it.

There is need-based aid for graduate students, but it usually comes in the form of federal student loans, which of course must be repaid, or federal work-study programs. A university bases its assessment of your need on the cost of attendance—the amount a graduate student spends on tuition, fees, books and supplies, transportation, living expenses, personal expenses, child care, credit card and other debt payments, summer costs, and miscellaneous expenses—minus the amount you (and your spouse, if you have one) can be expected to contribute. The resulting figure is your need. Any given school may or may not elect to or be able to give you enough aid to cover your need.

Many schools include a sample cost of attendance in their catalog or application packet, as shown below. When you apply for financial aid, you can use the sample as a basis to develop your own budget and cost of attendance. Note that most schools use a nine- or ten-month academic year as the basis of their cost of attendance. When you figure your own budget, you must account for your expenses during the summer months as well. See Appendix 1 for a blank budget and cost of attendance worksheet that you can use to estimate your own expenses.

Sample Costs of Attendance for a Single Student with No Dependents for Nine-Month Academic Year, at Private and Public Universities are as follows:

Costs	Private University	Public University, State Resident	Public University, Out-of-State Resident
Tuition	$20,250	$ 3,446	$ 9,850
Fees	$ 130	$ 1,790	$ 1,790
Books & supplies	$ 648	$ 720	$ 720
*Other expenses (housing, utilities, food, personal expenses, transportation, and miscellaneous)	$11,086	$ 9,700	$10,150
Total	$32,114	$15,656	$22,510

*This figure can vary considerably depending on your personal circumstances. Note that it does not include expenses for the summer months.

Internal Versus External Funding

Excluding loans, there are two basic sources of financial assistance for graduate students. The first is internal funding, which comes from the university, college, and department or program. This internal funding may take the form of fellowships, scholarships, grants, assistantships, work-study programs, and tuition waivers. If you receive any of this type of funding, you must use it at the school that awards it.

The second source of financial assistance is external funding, which comes from private foundations, corporations, and other organizations. External funding usually comes in the form of fellowships, scholarships, and grants. Each award has a purpose, usually to further research in a particular area or to promote the educational opportunities of a particular group, such as women and members of minority groups, often in a specific field. Some of the most well-known of the national fellowships come from the National Institutes of Health, the National Science Foundation, the Ford Foundation, and the Woodrow Wilson Fellowship Foundation, which awards Mellon Fellowships in the Humanities. You must apply for each fellowship individually to the awarding organization; your program application does not cover them. If you are awarded a fellowship, you may use it at whichever school you enroll in. If you receive a large external fellowship, graduate programs may find you a much more attractive candidate since the university or department need not use its own resources to fund you.

Most graduate students who receive non loan financial assistance receive it from their own departments and universities, not from outside sources. This fact should not discourage you from applying for external sources of funding if you think you qualify. However, the lion's share of your effort should be directed to making your program application outstanding, since that application is more likely to yield funding than applications to national fellowship programs.

Ph.D. Versus Master's Degree

Ph.D. candidates are not expected to be able to finance themselves for the six to ten years it may take to earn their degrees, and so in awarding financial aid, most programs give priority to doctoral candidates over master's candidates. If there's any money left after the doctoral candidates have been taken care of, then master's degree students may be given financial help. If this happens, then second-year master's students who have already proved themselves are more likely to be given financial assistance than incoming master's students. But in general, since their degrees take less time to earn, master's students are expected to pay for their graduate education themselves or borrow money if their own resources are insufficient.

Academic Versus Professional Degree

Most non-loan funding goes to doctoral candidates in academic fields. Students pursuing professional degrees, such as business, law, and medicine, do not generally receive merit-based funding, such as fellowships. In addition, their services as teaching assistants are not usually needed because courses at the professional schools are taught by professional faculty members. Instead, graduate students in most professional programs are expected to borrow if they need help paying for their education and living expenses.

One rationale for this is that professional students can expect to make large salaries after they receive their degrees. Therefore, accumulating debt is not as risky for them as it is for academic students, whose employment prospects are less certain and generally less remunerative.

Sciences and Engineering Versus Humanities and Arts

Students in the sciences and engineering are more likely to be generously funded than students in the humanities and arts. Professors in the sciences and engineering often have large, ongoing grants from the federal government or private organizations in order to conduct their research. Part of the grant money is often allocated to hiring graduate students as research assistants. At the large universities, students in the sciences may also receive teaching assistantships to help teach introductory science courses. There are more sources of external fellowships for science and engineering students, too, both from the federal government and private corporations.

> If you have been undecided about whether to pursue a master's degree or a doctoral degree, the issue of funding may be enough to tip the balance toward the doctoral degree. You'll have a much better chance of receiving funding if you apply as a doctoral candidate.

Full-Time Versus Part-Time Enrollment

Full-time students are more likely than part-time students to get financial assistance. Full-time students are seen as more committed to their educations, and they are not expected to work enough hours at an outside job to support themselves. Thus, a department or program usually funds the full-time students first. If there is money left, then part-time students may be given help.

Part-time students must be careful to understand the ramifications of their status on their eligibility for financial aid. The definition of part-time varies from university to university, and some forms of assistance, such as student loans, may require at least half-time enrollment. So if you are planning to borrow money, be sure you are taking enough courses to qualify for the loan program you have in mind.

Of course, there are financial advantages to attending part-time: You spread your costs out over a longer period, making them easier to pay. In addition, if you are working full-time while going to school part-time, your employer may reimburse part or all of your tuition.

Public Versus Private University

A top private university may have more resources with which to support its graduate students than a public university. If you think you have the academic credentials to be admitted to a program at one of the Ivy League schools or other top private institutions, then you should apply. If you are admitted, your chances of receiving adequate funding are good. On the other hand, the private universities usually have fewer undergraduates than the large public universities, so they have fewer teaching assistantships to award. In addition, if for some reason part or all of your funding is discontinued, you will be faced with the prospect of coming up with $25,000 to $30,000 per year.

The large public universities cost less than the private universities, especially for in-state residents. They have more teaching assistantships to offer because of the large number of undergraduates but fewer fellowships than the private universities. If you think you'll be financing all or most of your graduate education, attending a public university is the best way to reduce your costs—dramatically. Almost 70 percent of all graduate students attend public universities. They are getting a bargain.

In-State Versus Out-of-State Residency

If you are planning to attend a public university, your costs will be much lower if you are a state resident. For example, at the University of Michigan, full-time tuition for out-of-state graduate students is about $20,000 a year; for in-state residents it is about $10,000.

With so much money at stake, it is definitely worth your while to find out how you can establish residency in the state in which you are planning to get your graduate degree. You may simply have to reside in the state for a year—your first year of graduate school—in order to be considered a legal resident. Or, residence while a student may not count and you may have to move to the state a year before you plan to enroll. The legal residency requirements of each state vary, so be sure you have the right information.

TYPES OF FINANCIAL AID

Now that you have an overview of some of the factors involved in financial aid at the graduate level, let's examine the various types of aid that are available. The major types of financial aid for graduate students are fellowships and scholarships, assistantships, federal work-study and other work programs, loans, and tuition reimbursement.

Fellowships and Scholarships

Fellowships and scholarships are cash awards given by a department, university, or outside organization. They are usually awarded on the basis of merit, but some are awarded on the basis of need or are reserved for minority or women applicants. In addition, there are fellowships that are awarded simply because you have the particular qualifications that the philanthropist wanted to reward: for example, you are an Eagle Scout studying labor relations. (Needless to say, getting one of these is a long shot!) The words fellowship and scholarship are used somewhat interchangeably; there is no real difference between them, except that scholarships are usually awarded to undergraduates and fellowships to graduate students.

Fellowships are nice because, in return for the award, you are not expected to do anything but keep your grades up and make progress toward your degree. If the fellowship is substantial, it can free you to study and do research. If the fellowship is small, it may still add enough to your total aid package to enable you to attend school without borrowing. Fellowships may range from a low one-time award of $250 to a generous amount that covers tuition, fees, and living expenses and can be renewed for several years.

Many of the grants and fellowships that entering graduate students are eligible for have small cash awards, but you should consider applying for them anyway. First, any amount of money that you don't have to borrow is a plus, and small grants can add up. And second, having a history of receiving small fellowships will make your applications more attractive when you apply for the large fellowships in your later years of graduate school.

"At Penn State…I had to ask about fellowships," says Heather Helms-Erikson, who is earning a Ph.D. in human development and family studies. "I was very assertive—in fact, I hope I wasn't a pain in the neck. I made it very clear that I wasn't going unless I was fully funded," she recalls. "…I was offered a research assistantship and tuition waiver for the entire time…They nominated me for a university fellowship, and I got an additional $8,000 over two years. Since then, I've applied for every source of funding I can find."

Fellowships may be awarded by the department to which you are applying, the graduate school, the university, or an outside organization, such as the federal government or a private foundation. Your program application takes care of departmental fellowships, but if you are interested in pursuing other university fellowships, you will have to take the initiative, as Helms-Erikson did, and make inquiries at the department, graduate school, college, and financial aid offices. Likewise, applying for external fellowships is something you have to do on your own.

> **The words fellowship and scholarship are used somewhat interchangeably; there is no real difference between them except that scholarships are usually awarded to undergraduates and fellowships to graduate students.**

Assistantships

If you are offered an assistantship from the program or department to which you apply, you will be expected to work for the university in exchange for a stipend or salary, which is taxable. You may also receive a partial or full tuition waiver along with the assistantship. Most financial aid from large public universities is granted in the form of assistantships.

The value of assistantships varies widely from one university to another and from one field to another. In some cases, an assistantship along with a tuition waiver provides enough for you to go to school and pay your living expenses if you are single. "I had teaching assistantships and sometimes a research assistantship, plus a tuition waiver. I never had to pay anything," recalls a woman who earned a Ph.D. in Italian from a large, private Midwestern university. "What I received was enough to live on my own, although not always very comfortably." However, in other cases, an assistantship provides only partial funding and you will have to make up the balance of your school and living costs from other sources.

Not only do assistantships provide you with financial help, they may also draw you into the department's academic life because you are usually assigned to work with faculty members. "Assistantships are a source of professional development as well as funding," says Martha J. Johnson, Assistant Dean of the Graduate School at Virginia Tech. "An assistantship is a professional opportunity." There are three major types of assistantships: teaching, research, and administrative.

Teaching Assistantships

Large universities need many teaching assistants (TAs), particularly in departments like English and psychology, in which many undergraduates take courses. This is especially true of the large public universities, which rely heavily on TAs to teach or assist with introductory courses and lower-level undergraduate courses. Teaching assistantships are awarded by the department to which you are applying. As a TA, you usually help a professor by conducting small discussion classes, grading papers and exams, counseling students, and supervising laboratory groups. Some TAs teach a section of an introductory course, or are permitted to design and teach an upper-level course on their own. At many universities or departments, you will be given an orientation course to prepare you for teaching introductory classes, but at some institutions all you will get is on-the-job training. TAs usually work 15 to 20 hours a week, and, as a consequence, they may take a lighter course load.

Although working as a TA may slow down progress toward the degree, in most cases students feel that the experience they are gaining more than compensates for the extra time it takes to earn their degrees, especially if their ultimate goal is to teach at the university level. "I find that my teaching assistantship is extremely rewarding," says Cynthia Liutkus, a Ph.D. candidate in geology at Rutgers University in New Jersey. For teaching one course per semester, Liutkus receives a full tuition waiver and a stipend that covers fees, an off-campus apartment, and other living costs. Liutkus continues, "Not only does teaching provide me with the opportunity to strengthen my skills in the field of geology, but I enjoy interacting with the students. I hope that my enthusiasm for the subject is translated to them and hope they will continue on in the field." Liutkus recommends a teaching assistantship for any student who has an interest in teaching as a career. "Teaching... prepare[s] you for a number of things: information preparation and organization, public speaking, discipline, time management, etc. Graduate study will teach you all of these things as well, but teaching your own class sharpens your skills and makes you appreciate the dedication that your professors have for their work."

Some people consider teaching assistantships less attractive than fellowships because you must earn your money rather than getting it for "free." However, fellowship recipients lack the close contact with departmental faculty members and students that teaching assistants enjoy. This close contact helps TAs keep abreast of events and changes in their departments and makes it easier to know what's really going on. A teaching assistantship may also be a welcome change from the lonely life of doing solo research for many years. A department's TAs, who often share office space and take courses together, may find they enjoy the resulting camaraderie and competitive spirit.

Research Assistantships

A research assistant (RA) helps a faculty member with his or her research. Generally, research assistantships are awarded by a department and are paid for from grant money obtained by a professor from the federal government or private organizations. Some research assistantships are funded by university endowments or state money, and some are funded through grants obtained by the graduate student.

Most research assistantships are offered to students in the hard sciences and social sciences. An RA in the sciences works under the direction of a faculty member, assisting with laboratory research or field work. The professor who has the grant(s) gets to select the students he or she wants as RAs. If the professor is considering applicants to the department for the research assistantships, he or she generally chooses promising candidates with similar research interests.

There are also research assistantships in the humanities and arts, although they are fewer and tend to be of shorter duration and to have less monetary value. A humanities RA might perform research in libraries, assemble bibliographies, or check citations for a professor in the department. In many cases, you may be doing less rewarding clerical work, such as data entry or photocopying. Such research assistantships are rarely offered to incoming students but are given to students who have proven they have the ability or experience to do the job.

A research assistantship can be very rewarding or very frustrating. The benefit of receiving a research assistantship is that you are often able to work on research that is related to your own degree, especially if you are working with your adviser or mentor. Another bonus is that if you have done a lot of the research for a project, the faculty member may reward you with coauthorship of a publication—one of your first professional credentials. So if you've been matched up with a faculty member in your area of research interest or have the opportunity to work with other graduate students on a research team, the experience can be professionally rewarding. But if you are working for a faculty member whose interests do not match yours, a research assistantship helps pay your way but does not further your own educational or professional development.

Administrative Assistantships

Some schools offer assistantships in the university's administrative offices. You work 10 to 20 hours a week as an administrative assistant in one of the university's administrative or support services departments. Ideally, the work you do is related to your field of interest. For example, if you are a computer sciences student, you might do computer-related work for the university, or if you are a library and information sciences student, you might work in one of the university libraries.

Since administrative assistantships are sometimes outside your department and graduate school, they are often not awarded on the basis of your application, as are teaching and research assistantships. Instead, you have to look for them. You can find information about administrative assistantships in the school catalog or by contacting the university departments in which you'd like to work.

If You Are Offered an Assistantship

If you are offered an assistantship by a department or program, be sure to ask what the likelihood is that it will continue in subsequent academic years. Some programs routinely offer their assistantships to incoming students in order to get them to enroll; a year or two later, when the student is committed to the degree, they take away the assistantship and offer it to a new incoming student. So try to ascertain your chances of being funded for more than the first year or two.

You should also determine whether a full or partial tuition waiver comes with the assistantship. A tuition waiver is worth thousands of dollars and can make the difference between having enough to cover all your costs and scrambling to make up the shortfall.

Federal Work-Study and Other Work Programs

Federal Work-Study Program

Some universities participate in the federal work-study program, which provides students who demonstrate financial need with jobs in public and private nonprofit organizations. The government pays up to 75 percent of your wages and your employer pays the balance. The value of a work-study job depends on your need, the other elements in your financial aid package, and the amount of money the school has to offer. Not all universities have work-study funds, and some that do have the funds limit their use to undergraduates.

If you receive work-study funds, you may be able to use them in a job that relates to your field. You will have to check with the financial aid office to find out what jobs are available, whether you can use the funds in a job you find elsewhere, and what bureaucratic requirements you will have to satisfy.

Internships and Cooperative Education Programs

In addition to the federal work-study program, there are other employment opportunities that may help you finance your graduate education. Internships with organizations outside the university can provide money as well as practical experience in your field. As an intern, you are usually paid by the outside organization and you may or may not get credit for the work you do. Although they have been common in the professional programs, such as law and business, for years, internships lately have been growing in popularity in academic programs as well.

In cooperative education programs, you usually alternate periods of full-time work in your field with periods of full-time study. You are paid for the work you do, and you may or may not get academic credit for it as well.

> Internship and cooperative education programs may be administered in your department or by a separate university office, so you will have to ask to find out.

Loans

Unfortunately, at some point, most graduate students do have to take out loans to finance their education. Only wealthy students and Ph.D. students in certain fields are likely to be fully funded for the duration of their studies. Other students must borrow, whether they do it just one year to make up the amount not covered by other types of aid or whether they borrow each year to finance most of their graduate education, as some medical and law students do. Still, even if you expect to be making a huge salary after you receive your degree, it pays to minimize your debt if you can. Financial aid counselors recommend that your total student debt payment should not exceed 8 to 15 percent of your projected monthly income after you receive your degree.

Both graduate students and administrators have very strong opinions about loans. "I advise students not to take out loans if they can possibly help it," says Martha Johnson of Virginia Tech. "Consider the graduate student lifestyle as a short-term situation. If you are single, you can live in a dorm, use the university food service, sell your car, and concentrate on finishing as quickly as possible. With a simplified lifestyle, a single person can live on an assistantship." Denise Kaiser, who earned a Ph.D. in history from Columbia University, recalls how little money she had during her grad school years. "I remember someone suggesting dinner out, and I had to decline because money was tight...So I invited her over instead...I made something nice, like shrimp with pasta, and she was surprised that I could afford the ingredients. No matter how much the shrimp cost, it was still less than the price of an entree at a decent Manhattan restaurant, with carfare." Kaiser continues, "Boy, did I eat a lot of chicken during those years!... But the scrimping made it possible to afford my own place on a fellowship...I didn't borrow any money while I was at Columbia."

Jean Godby, a Ph.D. candidate in linguistics at Ohio State University, thinks that loans are a last resort for good reason. "All of my schooling was paid for by fellowships and assistantships. I was very leery of going into debt...," comments Godby. "I noticed that my friends who went into debt didn't like starting their work life with a financial burden." Another student, Tom Fuchs, who is earning a Psy.D. at the California School of Professional Psychology, had this comment: "Student loans are very appealing and often easy to get, but they accumulate very easily and are probably the major source of anxiety for students as they get closer to the end of the program." Fuchs adds, "I am glad I decided to continue to work, even though it means I will need more time to finish the program."

On the other hand, some students do not share this aversion to indebtedness. "I have tons of loans," says one student with a master's in education who is currently pursuing an Ed.D. "I have a student loan debt that is more than the value of my house at this point." Nestor Montilla, who is earning a master's degree in public administration from John Jay College of Criminal Justice in New York, also thinks loans are worth it. "If you have to take loans to get your education, do it," Montilla advises. "A federal loan is an investment in your education. You will pay later when you are a productive citizen."

In some situations, loans for graduate education may be forgiven. For example, under some programs, medical school loans may be forgiven if you work as a doctor in underserved areas. Check with the financial aid office to see if your situation may qualify.

Still others advised taking loans if necessary to get started, and then looking for other sources of funding once you have been in the program a short time. "I began paying for grad school with student loans, and I worked part-time to support myself," says Jenn Wagaman, a master's candidate in public communications at the University of Alaska at Fairbanks. "The second year, I got an assistantship." Kimani Toussaint, a Ph.D. candidate in electrical engineering at Boston University, adds: "Even if you have to take out loans during the first semester or year of graduate school, during that time you have the opportunity to approach many professors in your department to find out if they have any assistantships available or pending."

You can see that the question of taking out loans is more than just a calculation of present need and how much future indebtedness you can afford based on salary projections. It's also a question of your feelings about borrowing and your attitudes toward debt. In addition, your past credit history will affect whether or not you will be able to borrow. Thus, your decisions about whether and how much to borrow for your graduate education will be influenced by your past credit history, your financial calculations, and your attitudes toward debt.

If you decide to borrow, there are two basic sources of student loans: the federal government and private loan programs. If you are a homeowner, you might find it advantageous to use a home equity loan to help pay your educational costs. Whatever you do, do not use your credit cards to borrow money for school. The interest rates and finance charges will be astronomically high, and unless you can pay the balance in full, the charges will accrue rapidly.

Before tackling any loan application paperwork, you should make sure you meet the eligibility criteria. In addition, the terms of these loans will differ, so be sure to compare them, and make sure you understand what you are agreeing to before you sign on the dotted line. Keep in mind that most student loans have a guarantee fee (which insures the lender against your default) and an origination fee (which covers the administrative costs of the loan), both of which are a percentage of the amount you are borrowing. So, for example, if you are borrowing $5,000 with a guarantee fee of 1 percent and an origination fee of 3 percent, you will actually receive only $4,800.

Federal Student Loans

There are two basic types of loans offered to graduate students by the federal government: the Stafford loan (and the similar Direct Student Loan) and the Perkins loan. Up-to-date information about federal loan programs can be found at the Department of Education's Web site, http://www.ed.gov or by calling 800-4FEDAID (toll-free).

Stafford Loan Program

The federal government sponsors the Stafford Loan Program, which provides low-interest loans to graduate students through banks, credit unions, savings and loan institutions, and the universities themselves (through the Department of Education's Direct Lending Program). There are two types of Stafford loans:

Subsidized Stafford loan. To get a subsidized Stafford loan, you must demonstrate financial need. With a subsidized loan, the government pays the interest that is accruing while you are enrolled at least half-time in a graduate program.

Unsubsidized Stafford loan. If you cannot demonstrate financial need according to government criteria, you may still borrow, but your Stafford loan will be unsubsidized. This means you are responsible for paying the interest on the loan while you are still in school.

In both types of Stafford loans, repayment of the principal, as well as future interest, begins six months after you are last enrolled on at least a half-time basis. You may borrow up to $18,500 per year up to a maximum of $138,500, which includes any undergraduate loans you may still have. The interest rate varies annually and is set each July. Right now, it is capped at 8.25 percent.

Perkins Loan Program

Another source of federal funds is the Perkins Loan Program. The Perkins loan is available to students who demonstrate exceptional financial need and it is administered by the university itself. In some cases, universities reserve Perkins loans for undergraduates. If you are eligible for a Perkins loan, you may borrow up to $6,000 per year, up to a maximum of $40,000, including undergraduate borrowing. At present, the interest rate is 5 percent, and no interest accrues while you are enrolled in school at least half-time. You must start repaying the loan nine months after you are last enrolled on a half-time basis.

Consolidating Your Federal Loans

When you leave school (with a degree, we hope!), you can consolidate all your outstanding federal loans into one loan. Having one loan to repay will minimize the chances of administrative error and allow you to write one check per month rather than several.

Private Student Loans

In addition to the federal loan programs, there are many private loan programs that can help graduate students. Most private loan programs disburse funds based on your creditworthiness rather than your financial need. Some loan programs target all types of graduate students; others are designed specifically for business, law, or medical students. In addition, you can use other types of private loans not specifically designed for education to help finance your graduate degree. See Appendix 2 for sources of further information about these programs, or contact your school's financial aid office.

Graduate School Loans

There are many private loan programs designed to help graduate students in all fields. The loans are generally unsubsidized and your creditworthiness, as well as the limits of the program, will determine the amount you can borrow.

American Express Alternative Loan. This program is for students enrolled at least half-time in graduate school, and it is sponsored by American Express and the California Higher Education Loan Authority.

CollegeReserve Loan. Again, this loan program is for students enrolled at least half-time. It is sponsored by USA Group.

EXCEL Loan. This program, sponsored by Nellie Mae, is designed for students who are not ready to borrow on their own and wish to borrow with a creditworthy cosigner.

Graduate Access Loan. A loan program, sponsored by the Access Group, for graduate students enrolled at least half-time.

Signature Student Loan. A loan program, sponsored by Sallie Mae, for students who are enrolled at least half-time.

Business School Loans

There are several loan programs designed for students pursuing graduate degrees in business.

Business Access Loan Program. This loan program, sponsored by the Access Group, allows student to borrow a maximum of $120,000 in total outstanding educational debt. Students attending less than half-time may borrow the cost of tuition, fees, and up to $500 for books and supplies.

M.B.A. Loans and the Tuition Loan Plan (TLP). This is a loan program designed for students who are attending graduate schools of business on more than a half-time basis. You may borrow up to $13,500 per year, with a limit of $25,000; total unpaid educational loans from all sources cannot exceed $60,000.

MBASHARE. MBASHARE, a loan program offered by the New England Loan Marketing Association (Nellie Mae), allows students to borrow up to $15,000 without a cosigner, and up to the cost of attendance with a cosigner, to a maximum of $80,000. A parent or other fiscally responsible person can be the primary borrower.

Law School Loans

Among the private loan programs designed for law students are the following:

- *Law Access Loan.* The Access Group sponsors a program for law students in which you may borrow federal Stafford loans or private loans up to a maximum total outstanding educational debt of $120,000. In addition, they provide a loan designed to cover your expenses during the period in which you are studying for the bar examination.
- *LawLoans.* LawLoans offers federal Stafford loans, a private Law Student Loan (LSL), and a Bar Study Loan. You may borrow up to $15,000 per year, up to a maximum of $60,000 ($100,000 with a cosigner).
- *LawSHARE.* This program, sponsored by Nellie Mae, allows you to borrow up to $15,000 without a cosigner, and up to the cost of attendance with a cosigner, to a maximum of $80,000. A parent or other fiscally responsible person can be the primary borrower.

Medical School Loans

It is common for medical students to begin their careers with debts over $100,000. For most medical students, the large debt is justified by the high incomes they can expect to earn. Among the medical school loan programs are:

- *AAMC MedLoans.* The Association of American Medical Colleges offers the Alternative Loan Program (ALP). Under this program, you may borrow up to $30,000 per year, up to a total debt of $120,000. Payment during your postgraduate training period can be deferred for up to three or four years.
- *Medical Access Loans.* This program, sponsored by the Access Group, allows you to borrow up to a cumulative total educational debt of $165,000. Payment can be deferred until you complete a required residency program.
- *MedSHARE.* Nellie Mae offers a loan program to medical and dental students that allows you to borrow up to $20,000 without a cosigner and up to the cost of attendance with a cosigner. Your cumulative debt can be no more than $120,000 if you are a medical student or $90,000 if you are a dental student. A parent or other fiscally responsible person can be the primary borrower.

Home Equity Loans

For students who own their own homes, a home equity loan or line of credit can be an attractive financing alternative to private loan programs. Some of these loans are offered at low rates and allow you to defer payment of the principal for years. In addition, if you use the loan to pay for educational expenses, the interest on the loan is tax deductible.

Tuition Reimbursement

If you are working full-time and attending school part-time, you may be reimbursed for part or all of your tuition by your employer. "I receive tuition reimbursement through my company," says Andrea Edwards Myers, who is earning a Master of Arts in public communications on a part-time basis from the College of St. Rose in Albany, New York. "They offer a capped total of $3,000 a year for tuition...One thing to be aware of, however, is that the federal government taxes graduate tuition reimbursement money, so you will receive a reduced amount in your check. The balance, therefore, is up to you to make up when paying the college." Check with your employer before you enroll; some employers reimburse tuition only for job-related courses.

IF YOU ARE A WOMAN, MINORITY STUDENT, OR VETERAN...

There are many sources of financial assistance that target qualified women, minority, or veteran graduate students. For women, much of this aid is available for graduate study in fields in which women have been traditionally underrepresented, in particular, the physical sciences and engineering. For example, in the physical sciences, fewer than one third of the graduate students are women. In engineering, fewer than one fifth are women. To help achieve a gender balance in these fields, many fellowship programs are offered only to qualified women. For instance, the Zonta International Foundation offers fellowships for study in aerospace-related sciences or engineering, and the National Science Foundation offers special grants to women studying in the sciences, engineering, or mathematics.

In addition, there are funds earmarked for women in other fields of study. For example, the American Association of University Women awards several grants and fellowships each year to women pursuing graduate study in any field, and the Women's Research and Education Institute offers fellowships for study in fields related to public policy.

Qualified minority students are in great demand in graduate schools in all fields. Historically, minority students have been under-represented at the graduate level, and there are now many programs that seek to increase the number of minority students by offering financial assistance. The federal government has established a number of programs that award grants and fellowships to qualified minority students. The Indian Fellowship Program, Minority Access to Research Careers, and the National Science Foundation Minority Graduate Fellowships are just a few examples of federal programs that target minority students. In addition, many private and corporate sponsors have developed programs to help minority students finance their graduate education. These include the American Fund for Dental Health, the American Geological Institute, the American Planning Association, and the Ford Foundation, among others.

Veterans who have contributed to one of the Veteran Educational Benefits programs are entitled to use their benefits for graduate education. You do not have to show financial need to participate in one of these programs; they are a benefit of your service in the armed forces. The amount of assistance you will receive depends on length of service, the number of dependents you have, and the number of courses you are taking.

There are many resources you can use to find targeted assistance for women, members of minority groups, and veterans. You'll find some resources that will get you started in Appendix 2.

IF YOU ARE AN INTERNATIONAL STUDENT...

Unfortunately, financial assistance for international students is limited. About 75 percent of international students do not receive any aid from U.S. sources. If you are an international student, you do not qualify to receive federal loans or work-study assistance; although if you can find a willing and creditworthy U.S. citizen to cosign a loan, you may be able to borrow from the private loan programs described above. If you do get financial help, it is likely to come from the department or program in which you are enrolled, although there are some government programs that underwrite graduate students to promote cultural exchange.

Finding help to finance your graduate education is a challenge, but it's not impossible. You can start at home by contacting your country's U.S. educational advising center, which can help you identify institutions that fund international students. Check Appendix 2 for further sources of information about aid for international students.

LOCATING INFORMATION ABOUT FINANCIAL AID

Finding information about financial aid is a challenge. There is no central clearinghouse for information about financial aid for graduate study. You are going to have to check a number of different sources to get the full picture on possible sources of aid for you. We'll discuss a few of them here, but see Appendix 2 for a list of financial aid resources.

The University

Even at the university, there is more than one source of information about financial aid. Each university has a different administrative structure, so you will have to figure out the offices you will need to contact. These may include:

- *The program or department to which you are applying.* Often the program brochures describe the types of funding that the department awards its students. If you cannot find this information in the printed materials you've been sent, then call the program and ask. You'll be able to find out about departmental assistantships and fellowships from this source.
- *The financial aid office.* The financial aid office is generally the best source of information about federal and private loan programs as well as work-study assistance. They may also be able to steer you to other sources of information.
- *The college's administrative office.* The next place to check is the college's administrative office. For example, you may be applying for a Ph.D. in English literature. The English department is likely to be under the jurisdiction of the College of Arts and Sciences. That office may or may not administer fellowships and grants to the students of the college. Call them to find out.
- *The office of the graduate school.* This is another administrative office that may or may not have funding to award. If they do, the fellowships or grants are likely to be awarded on a university-wide competitive basis.

It's important to check with all these offices to see what's available. "A program's general tendency is to broadcast news of outside fellowships but keep close to the vest about its own funds," says Jonathan Roberts, Manager of Enrollment Services at Pepperdine University's Graduate School of Education and Psychology in California. "Students need to be proactive and call the program as well as the financial aid office to find out their chances of receiving aid."

Many agencies of the federal government offer fellowships to graduate students in related fields. Contact the agencies that are relevant to your field of study for further information.

The Government

A good source of information on federal aid for graduate students is the federal government itself. Most need-based aid is administered by the Department of Education. You can contact them through their Web site, by telephone, or by mail (see Appendix 2 for specifics). Remember, however, that not all universities participate in each federal program, so if a particular program interests you, you will have to contact the university financial aid office to make sure it's available.

It also pays to check whether your state offers support to graduate students. Some states, like California, New York, Michigan, Oklahoma, and Texas have large aid programs for their residents. Other states may have little or nothing to offer. Contact your state scholarship office directly to find out what's available and whether you are eligible to apply.

The Internet

The Internet is an excellent source of information about all types of financial aid. One of the best places to start your Internet search for financial aid is the Financial Aid Information Page at http://www.finaid. org. This site has a great deal of information about the different types of financial aid and provides links to other relevant sites as well. It provides a good overview of the financial aid situation. In addition, the site offers several calculators that enable you to estimate many useful figures, including projected costs of attendance, loan payments, and the amount you will be expected to contribute to your education and living expenses if you are applying for need-based aid.

There are also a number of searchable databases of national scholarships and fellowships on the Internet. The best known of these is FastWeb at http://www.fastweb.com. It takes about half an hour to answer the FastWeb questionnaire about your educational background, field of study, and personal characteristics. When you are done, FastWeb searches its database to match your data with eligibility requirements of several hundred thousand fellowships and scholarships. You are then given a list of possible fellowships and scholarships to pursue on your own. There is no cost for this service.

There are a few things you should beware of when using Internet search services. First, a searchable database is only as good as its index, so you may find yourself getting some odd matches. In addition, most searchable databases of scholarships and fellowships are designed primarily for undergraduates, so the number of potential matches for a graduate student is far fewer than the several hundred thousand sources of aid that a database may contain. Finally, some of these Internet search services charge a fee. Given the amount of free information that's available, both on the Internet and in libraries, it's not necessary to pay for this type of research.

Print Directories

Although the searchable databases on the Internet are easy to use, it's still a good idea to check print directories of national fellowships, grants, and scholarships. These directories have indexes that make locating potential sources of funds easy. Fellowships and grants are indexed by field of study as well as by type of student. So, for example, you can search for all funding related to the study of Latin America or landscape architecture. Or you can search for funding that is targeted to Hispanic students, disabled students, or entering students. It's a good idea just to browse, too, in case something catches your eye.

There are quite a few directories that you can consult. *The Annual Register of Grant Support: A Directory of Funding Sources*, published by the National Register Publishing Company, is a comprehensive guide to awards from the government, foundations, and business and professional organizations. *Peterson's Grants for Graduate and Postdoctoral Study* is a directory of 1,400 fellowships and scholarships that covers all fields of study. There are also directories that specialize in fellowships for particular fields of study and for particular types of students.

APPLYING FOR FINANCIAL AID

Depending on your personal situation and the requirements of the graduate school, you may have to submit just one or a number of applications for financial aid. The simplest situation is that of a student applying only for merit-based departmental or program funding. If that's your case, you may need to submit only the program application and that will take care of the departmental funding as well. However, if you are applying for need-based aid, university fellowships, national fellowships, or private loan programs, you will have several application forms to deal with. However many applications you must submit, start the process early.

Timetable

"I cannot overemphasize the importance of applying early," says Emerelle McNair, Director of Scholarships and Financial Aid at Southern Polytechnic State University in Georgia. "Most awards are made in spring for the following academic year." Be sure you've picked the correct deadlines from your program application information packet. Students applying for financial aid often have an earlier deadline for the entire application.

If you are looking for sources of funding outside the program and university, such as national fellowships, then it is even more important to start early—a full year or more before you plan to enroll. "You have to do your program applications concurrently with your fellowship applications," advises Martha J. Johnson, Assistant Dean of the Graduate School at Virginia Tech. "Everything is due around the same time."

Remember, it can easily take months to fill out applications and assemble all the supporting data for a financial aid request. You may need to submit income tax forms, untaxed income verification, asset verification, and documents that support any special circumstances you are claiming. Give yourself plenty of time to submit the initial application. Later, if you are asked to provide additional information or supporting documents by the financial aid office, do so as quickly as possible.

The Program Application

For many graduate schools, the program application is the main financial aid application as well. As we have mentioned before, much of the funding for incoming graduate students is determined by the admissions committee's assessment of the merit of program applications.

> Students applying for financial aid often have an earlier deadline for the entire application.

So a strong program application, submitted on time, will improve your chances of getting funding from your department. Remember that you cannot predict which elements of your application will be weighted most heavily by a given admissions committee, so do your best on all of them.

"I was offered a scholarship to attend my program based on my previous experience as well as my personal essays," says Felecia Bartow, an M.S.W. candidate at Washington University in St. Louis. "Put a lot of time and effort into your personal essays as they are often used to award scholarship money." Other students suspected that their GRE scores helped them get aid. You'll probably never know on what basis the funding decisions were made.

School's Financial Aid Application Form

In addition to the program application, there may be a separate financial aid application. This will often be the case if you are applying for need-based aid. If you do not see such a form in the program application packet, call the graduate school to find out whether you need to obtain it from another office.

Some schools require you to submit a standardized form, the College Scholarship Service's (CSS) Financial Aid PROFILE. This form is similar to the FAFSA, described below, but it is used to award university aid.

FAFSA

You may remember the Free Application for Federal Student Aid (FAFSA) form from your undergraduate days. FAFSA is also used by graduate students who are applying for need-based federal aid, such as the federal loan programs and work-study. The FAFSA form is issued annually by the Department of Education right after New Year's Day (see http://www.fafsa.ed.gov). On it, you report financial data from the previous year in order to be considered for aid in the school year starting the following fall. It's much easier to fill out the FAFSA if you have already done your federal income tax forms for the year.

For purposes of need-based federal financial aid, all graduate students are considered financially independent of their parents. Because the FAFSA is designed for undergraduate students who are dependent

> Remember that you cannot predict which elements of your application will be weighted most heavily by a given admissions committee, so do your best on all of them.

You can do a rough calculation of your Estimated Family Contribution, the amount you will be expected to contribute to your education in a given year. All you need is your previous year's tax return and a program's cost of attendance figures. Use one of the EFC calculators on the Internet, such as the one at http://www.finaid.org.

on their parents, you may find you are having difficulty interpreting some of the questions or that the questions do not cover all your circumstances. If there is information about your financial situation that is not elicited by the FAFSA but that you feel is germane to your application, then explain the circumstances in a separate letter to the financial aid office. Suppose, for example, that you have been working full-time for a few years but you are planning to quit your job and attend graduate school full-time. You would complete the FAFSA using the previous year's full-time income figures, but this would not be an accurate reflection of your financial situation during the following school year because your income will drop precipitously. In such a case, you would notify the financial aid office so that they can make a professional judgment as to whether your need should be revised upward.

After you submit the FAFSA, you will receive an acknowledgment that includes a summary of the data you have sent them. Check to make sure the information is accurate and that the schools you have chosen to have the data sent to are correctly listed. If there are errors, make corrections right away. Your acknowledgment will also show your Expected Family Contribution, the amount you and your spouse can be expected to contribute. This information is used by each school to calculate your need (cost of attendance minus Expected Family Contribution) and to award need-based aid.

You can do a rough calculation of your Estimated Family Contribution, the amount you will be expected to contribute to your education in a given year. All you need is your previous year's tax return and a program's cost of attendance figures. Use one of the EFC calculators on the Internet, such as the one at http://www.finaid.org.

Fellowship Applications

If you are applying for university or national fellowships, you will have to submit separate applications for each one to the awarding organizations. Follow instructions carefully, making sure you meet all deadlines. Fellowship applications can be as elaborate as program applications, with letters of recommendation and essays, so allow yourself a lot of time to complete them.

Following Up

Just as you do with your program application, follow up with your financial aid applications as well. If you do not receive an acknowledgment that your FAFSA form was received within a couple of weeks, check on its status. In addition, call the university offices with which you are dealing to make sure everything is proceeding smoothly. "Politely check on your application every so often—making as many friends as you can in the process," recommends Neill Kipp, a Ph.D. candidate in computer science at Virginia Tech. "As with any large organization, things fall in the cracks. Having friends in the financial aid office, your own academic department, and the graduate school helps immensely."

PAYING FOR GRADUATE SCHOOL IS POSSIBLE

You can see that it is possible to find the financial aid that will help you pay for graduate school. You will have to be persistent in your search for funds, may have to spend months working on financial aid research and applications, and may have to borrow money. And once you enter a graduate program you may have to simplify your lifestyle in order to cut your expenses.

But if you really want to go to graduate school, you can find the financial help that will make it possible. Be realistic about your needs, leave yourself enough time to complete all the paperwork, and do your homework. Now is a good time to look back on all the reasons you want to attend graduate school—to remind yourself why it's worth it.

Making Your Final Choice

Your time and effort have paid off, and those thick acceptance packages have begun arriving in the mail. If you are admitted by your first-choice program—and you can afford to attend—then there's no further debate: you will enroll. But if you are accepted by more than one program and you are undecided, you'll have to make a choice. At this point, visiting the institutions, even if you have done so in the past, can help you make up your mind. Now that the program has indicated its interest in you, you should be able to have an even more fruitful exchange with professors, students, and administrators.

VISITING THE CAMPUS

To illustrate how important campus visits can be, even after you are admitted, consider the experience of Jean Godby, who dropped out of a Ph.D. program in linguistics in the 1980s and then resumed her studies in the same program more than ten years later. She recalls that when she first enrolled in 1978, she had not visited the campus. "I was shocked when I figured out after being at Ohio State for one week that the morale was low and many people were thinking about dropping out." She suggests, "Visit the school and talk to current students."

Maria Vesperi, Associate Professor of Anthropology at New College, the honors college of Florida's state university system, advises her undergraduates to make campus visits. "Students should make a personal visit—but make an appointment ahead of time," says Vesperi. "I've had some students report that there was no one around when they visited a school." So call the graduate adviser of the department at least a week in advance to set up interviews with faculty members and students.

In addition, try to arrange a campus tour with a graduate student in circumstances similar to yours. For example, if you are married and have young children, ask to be guided by a married student with children. That way, you'll get a more accurate impression of the institution in terms of your family situation. If the university has a graduate student association, you can call them to ask whether one of their members can show you around or meet with you at the end of your visit.

When you visit, keep in mind that the program has decided it wants you. The people you meet officially are likely to be wooing you, especially if you have other offers. For example, Kimberly Tremblay was accepted by half a dozen programs in biology. "They each paid for me to go out and interview," says Tremblay. "That was critical in my decision. I liked Penn because the people were so diverse. I was still unsure of which lab I wanted to work in, and there were lots of choices." Tremblay may have enjoyed being wooed, but she still made her decision to enroll in the University of Pennsylvania's Ph.D. program on the basis of its research opportunities.

Interviewing Faculty

You should have increased access to the professors in the program now that you have been accepted. Before you meet them for interviews, get copies of the professors' curriculum vitae, which may be posted on the program's Web site or available from the program's office. If you have time, read a couple of the faculty member's most recent articles so you will be familiar with his or her research.

If you know which faculty members you are likely to be working closely with, now is the time to assess them more closely. Are the faculty members glad to talk to you? Are your interests really a good match for theirs? How do their graduate students fare? Do their students receive their degrees in a timely fashion, or are they enmeshed in one further revision after another? Do you think you can get along with them? If you are enrolling in a program that involves research and a thesis, do not underestimate the importance of the personal relationships that will develop between you and your faculty advisers. As a graduate student, you are often an apprentice to your professors. Your relationships with them can influence the course of your studies as well as your professional future.

Try to arrange a campus tour with a graduate student in circumstances similar to yours.

For that reason, it's important to discover, if you can, the plans of the professors with whom you would like to work. "The makeup of a department can change rapidly because of retirement and financial instability," says Jay Sokolovsky, Professor of Anthropology at the University of South Florida. "Try to find out whether the faculty members in whom you are interested are likely to be there over the course of your education."

During the interview, unless the professor clearly enjoys talking to you about your interests, the program, or his or her own research, don't take up too much of his or her time. Instead, ask whether the professor can recommend some graduate students with whom you can speak. You'll get a different perspective on these professors and the program from their students.

Talking to Graduate Students

Check out the faculty members and the department by getting the points of view of several graduate students as well. "Talk with the grad students," suggests a Ph.D. candidate in physics at Harvard University, "to find out how happy they are with their choice." Be sure to talk to more than one person to get a good perspective on the faculty and the program. Find out whether funding is likely to continue after the first year. Ask what graduates of the department do after they earn their degrees. In addition to talking with students you meet through the graduate adviser, try to find other students of the program to get a more balanced view.

When you talk with students, you may sometimes have to probe a bit to be able to assess what you are hearing. "I...talked to doctoral students in the program," explains Cathy Chappell, who is pursuing an Ed.D. at the University of Cincinnati. "Actually, many of them were negative, but when I pressed them for the reasons, I realized that the things they did not like would be positives for me or would have little impact on me." So be sure not to take everything you hear at face value. Ask follow-up questions about matters that are important to you.

> "We send prospective students out to lunch with other students," says Gail Ashley, Professor of Geological Sciences at Rutgers University in New Jersey. "We want them to know what we're really like, because we're not going to change!"

Meeting the Department's Administrative Staff

Ask to be introduced to the department's administrative staff. These people, who run the department on a daily basis, have a good perspective on the personalities and activities of the various professors and graduate students and the procedures of the department and university. In other words, the administrative staff can be a valuable source of information and assistance to you as a graduate student, or they can be unforthcoming and uncooperative. Try to assess the staff members' attitudes when you meet them.

Visiting Libraries and Labs

"Check out the facilities, especially the library," recommends Stephanie Muntone, who earned a master's degree in history and a certificate in archival management from New York University. "You don't want to have to study in oppressive surroundings." Find out whether the library has a good collection of sources related to your field and whether graduate students have special privileges with regard to borrowing regular items and using special collections.

If you are a student in the hard sciences or engineering, ask to take a tour of the labs. You'll be spending a lot of time in the labs, especially if you have been offered a research assistantship, so check out the environment and the attitudes of the professors and students you meet.

Assessing Student Services

In addition to checking out the faculty members, students, department, and research facilities, evaluate the student services provided by the university. "Visit the campus, and talk to as many people as you can. Don't be afraid to ask how thing are there," advises a Harvard University student. "Pay particular attention to how well the grad students are treated on an institutional level." Nestor Montilla, a master's candidate in public administration at John Jay College in New York, also thinks that student services are important. "Make an overall assessment of the different offices students have to deal with...to make a judgment about the quality of services provided," he suggests.

Now might be a good time to visit the housing office, for example, and take a look at the university housing that's available for graduate students. Check out the computer facilities and Internet access. If you are a minority or international student, find out if there are offices or organizations on campus that offer student services and an opportunity to socialize. If you are receiving need-based aid, visit the financial aid office. Ask other graduate students their opinions of university student services.

Evaluating the Community

Finally, take a close look at the community in which you will be living. Is the area rural or urban? Provincial or cosmopolitan? Homogeneous or diverse? Walk or drive around. Will you enjoy living here? Are the neighborhood and campus pleasant, safe environments? Can you afford to live here? Will you need a car? Look at the housing ads and the employment ads. Find out about the local day care or school system if you have children. Read the local newspaper and watch the news on TV. You can learn a lot about a community from the local media.

Evaluating Your Campus Visit

Prospective students who have been out in the work force for several years tend to view themselves, at least in part, as consumers, and they evaluate what they glean from their campus visits from that perspective. "After all, you are the one doing the hiring," comments Neill Kipp, a Ph.D. candidate in computer science at Virginia Tech. A Simmons College student pursuing a master's degree in library and information science agrees. "I believe that graduate students should be treated respectfully and well as scholars and consumers by their institutions. This treatment usually determines whether graduates will remain interested and active with the institution in the future." One master's candidate in orientation mobility and rehabilitation teaching at Hunter College in New York said simply, "Let the buyer beware."

The consumer perspective comes more easily to students who are financing their own educations. However, even if you are being funded, thinking as a consumer can shed a new light on the programs you are considering. Although it may be hard to change your perspective from applicant (or supplicant) to buyer or to think of a graduate education as a big-ticket consumer item, once you've been accepted to a program, the balance has shifted. Now you are the one making the decision.

NEGOTIATING THE BEST DEAL

After you've made a closer assessment of the programs to which you have been accepted, you may still be torn—usually because of a discrepancy in level of funding. For example, your first choice may not have offered you full funding, but your second choice did. What should you do?

Double-Checking Your Figures

Don't be shy about asking for more funding. If what is keeping you from accepting your first choice program is inadequate funding, call the graduate adviser and explain your situation.

First, be absolutely sure what you are being offered in the way of funding. A few departments admit students first and award funding later, so if your letter of acceptance does not mention funding, it's a good idea to call the program and find out whether funding is still being awarded. If you have been awarded funding, such as a teaching assistantship, is it clear whether a tuition waiver is part of the deal? Reread your acceptance letters, and call the departments and the financial aid offices to clarify anything that puzzles you. Double-check all the figures and be sure you know the total value of the funding package and the amount, if any, you will have to contribute.

Asking for More

Don't be shy about asking for more funding. If what is keeping you from accepting your first choice program is inadequate funding, call the graduate adviser and explain your situation. They may be able to offer you more departmental funding, for example, because more applicants have turned them down than they originally anticipated, freeing up assistantships. They may be able to nominate you for competitive university-wide fellowships. Or they may be able to suggest alternative sources of aid, such as federal loans. If you have done your homework on sources of financial aid (see Chapter 8), you will be in a better position to ask the right questions and get the best deal.

Waiting Until the Deadline

Don't rush to accept any offers. Almost all major university programs abide by an agreement created by the Council of Graduate Schools to hold offers of financial assistance open until April 15 for fall enrollment.

So there is no point in sending in an early acceptance if you are still waiting for other offers to come in or negotiating with a department to get a better offer. However, even though this is in conflict with the agreement, some programs may ask for an earlier decision in order to fill slots and send out another round of acceptances before April 15. If this is the case and the university is a signatory to the agreement, you can accept the offer early and then withdraw your acceptance in writing before April 15. Although this is in conformity with the letter of the agreement, it's not a very good way to do business, so try to avoid this situation if you can.

It's usually better to wait, as difficult as that may be. For example, Cindy Liutkus was torn when her first choice, Rutgers, offered her a teaching assistantship that was only half-time. "Don't feel rushed to make a decision," Liutkus advises. "I was convinced that Rutgers would not be able to give me the full teaching assistantship that I was hoping for, and therefore, even though I wanted to attend, I considered taking another offer in Boston for financial reasons. I was concerned that if I waited too long to make my decision that I would miss my chance," adds Liutkus. However, she did wait until all her offers were in, and at the last minute Rutgers offered her a full assistantship. She accepted their offer.

Making Tradeoffs

You may be unable to persuade your first-choice program to improve its offer of aid. In that case, you will have to decide whether you should accept their offer anyway and borrow the balance of what you need or decline the offer and attend a program that's offered you more money. In this situation, most students opt for the program with the best funding package. "When choosing a...program, the three most important things are support, support, and support," says Renee Lantz, a Ph.D. candidate in fire protection engineering at Worcester Polytechnic Institute in Massachusetts. "Obtaining an advanced degree is a highly stressful pursuit. Financial support is the greatest asset you can have." Neill Kipp, a Ph.D. candidate in computer science at Virginia Tech, agrees. "Finding an income stream that is steady and stress-free is important," says Kipp. "Worrying about finding consulting clients is no way to spend the week before midterms." As important as money is, only you can decide whether it's the overriding factor.

FOLLOWING YOUR INSTINCTS

The graduate students we surveyed for this book were generally quite rational in their approach to graduate school, and many of them explained—very logically—the various factors they evaluated when deciding which graduate program to accept. As you might expect, the availability of funding seemed to be the major deciding factor for many of them. Still, it was interesting to note that the word instincts came up quite a few times in this context. After weighing the pros and cons of each program pretty systematically, many students said that they followed their instincts, choosing the school that felt right for them. "I followed my instincts...and chose to attend (in part) based on the supportiveness exhibited by both faculty and staff with whom I had contact prior to my enrollment," explains Felecia Bartow, an M.S.W. candidate at Washington University in St. Louis. When asked what advice she would give prospective students about selecting a graduate program, Megan McAfee, an M.F.A. candidate in costume technology at Virginia Tech, said simply, "Go with your instincts." Is that good advice for you? Perhaps, but only if your instincts are backed up by what you've learned about the program in the course of researching, applying, and visiting.

IF YOU DON'T GET IN

It's possible that you will not get in to any of the programs to which you apply. If this happens to you, don't assume that your graduate education has ended before it's even begun. And don't jump to the conclusion that your own "inferiority" has placed you in this position. In Chapter 6, we discussed the difficulty of predicting on what bases any given admissions committee makes its decisions. You may have been turned down for any number of reasons, from the lack of a match between your interests and the faculty's to an unusually large applicant pool in your area that year.

On the other hand, this is a good opportunity to reexamine your applications and identify any weaknesses. Were your graduate admissions test scores less than stellar? Do you suspect that one of your letters of recommendation might have been lukewarm? Was your personal essay too general to demonstrate your interest in a particular program? You can even write to each program and ask them why you were not admitted and how you can strengthen a future application. They may not tell you exactly why you were not accepted, but they may offer you advice on shoring up any weak aspects of your application. Or you may find out that your area of interest had an unusual number of applicants that year and you should simply try again.

You may also need to reevaluate the programs to which you applied. If they are out of your reach for good reason, then you may have to go through the research and selection process again to find more suitable programs. You'll find it's easier to apply to a second round of programs because by then, you will be a pro!

The Graduate School Experience

Congratulations! You have weathered the selection and application process, and you are about to embark on your graduate education. As you will soon find out for yourself, graduate school is not like college and it's not like work. The experience is quite different in many respects. In graduate school, you will be expected to work independently, take the initiative in your studies, and monitor your own progress. You'll have more work to accomplish in less time than you would think possible. On the other hand, you will be doing work you enjoy, with people who share your enthusiasm. And you will be making rewarding progress toward your goals.

MAKING THE ADJUSTMENT

For many students, the first semester of graduate school is extremely difficult. From the familiar routine of college life or a job, you are plunged into a strange and intense new environment in which you are not quite sure what's expected of you, but you are quite sure that it's a lot. According to Gail Ashley, Professor of Geological Sciences at Rutgers University in New Jersey, a student's transition to graduate school will be easier if he or she is organized. "Students need to have their personal lives in order so they can concentrate on their studies," says Ashley. Adjusting to graduate school may mean overcoming fears of intellectual inadequacy, getting used to life on a big campus, or giving up the free time you've gotten used to as a working person.

From College to Graduate School

Many students are surprised at how differently undergraduates and graduate students approach their studies. As an undergraduate, you are expected to sample a wide range of disciplines and spend a considerable amount of time on extracurricular activities and your social life. In graduate school, however, the emphasis shifts. You are now expected to be focused and professional in your outlook. "Graduate school is completely different from undergraduate school," says Kimani Toussaint, a Ph.D. candidate in electrical engineering at Boston University. "Undergraduate school, for me, was sort of the transition from youth to adulthood. The whole experience, especially because I lived on campus, was more than just the classes. I learned a lot from other students, both in and out of class, about life in general." Toussaint continues, "By the time I started graduate school, I was ready to approach the whole experience as a job. I enjoyed it a lot. I was a lot more focused in the classes than I was [as an] undergrad, and I was completely surprised by the amount that I learned in just a few years."

Stephanie Muntone, who earned a master's degree in history and a certificate in archival management from New York University, also remembers the contrast between college and graduate school. "In college, classes were not that difficult...but at NYU, the readings were difficult and advanced. The attitude was, you are now a professional, not a kid, and you are expected to do just what you need to do. People were there to work," says Muntone. "We had fun, but the attitude was very different from the attitude in college."

Nestor Montilla, who came to the United States from the Dominican Republic as a young man, was surprised by the dramatic increase in intellectual rigor that he encountered when he reached graduate school. "[As an undergraduate], I felt I was not challenged enough, although I had to learn a new language. Some classes seemed to be customized to the level of students who were not ready for college work. This is why I thought some classes were 'empty' or too 'lax.'" Montilla, who is earning a master's degree in public administration at John Jay College of Criminal Justice in New York, continues, "At John Jay College, I then knew what academic rigor was like. Reading assignments seemed almost impossible to complete. Time was not enough to finish all the assigned homework. In addition, I noticed that students at John Jay College were more academically prepared. I had to compete against them for class participation. I also learned to be careful about expressing my ideas and to be prepared for class."

> "It took me a while to realize that I wasn't expected to know everything. I started out being afraid to ask questions, and before I knew it, I couldn't stop asking questions."

When she entered the doctoral program in geology at Rutgers University, Cindy Liutkus was nervous about looking ignorant and foolish in comparison with her fellow graduate students. "I guess the biggest adjustment was overcoming the fear of not knowing enough. It's intimidating to come out of an undergraduate institution and immediately enter the graduate realm, with students who may have been in graduate school for many years and others who may have worked in the field for years before returning to school," says Liutkus. "It took me a while to realize that I wasn't expected to know everything," she continues. "I started out being afraid to ask questions, and before I knew it, I couldn't stop asking questions."

Not only is the work more difficult and the competition from fellow students more intense, but graduate school is also much more time consuming. Gone are the days when you could leave exam and paper preparation to the last minute. There is simply too much to do. "Graduate school is much more demanding than college," says Tammy Hammershoy, an M.A. candidate in English at Western Connecticut State University. "You should be enrolled only if you are serious about it; otherwise it is a waste of money and time. For me, the most difficult adjustment was the increase in reading, papers, and projects. This, plus work, left very little time for other things. It is definitely a commitment."

Jennifer Cheavens, who is working on a Ph.D. in clinical psychology at the University of Kansas at Lawrence, found that the most important difference between college and graduate school is her professors and fellow students. "First, grad school is different from college because the people who are around you are different. Everyone is interested in similar topics and so there is some sort of uniting experience there. Also, most people are pretty motivated and work pretty hard." Cheavens continues, "Second, there is just more work. More reading, more writing." She concludes, "Third, there are (at least in my field) more divergent expectations. In addition to course work, you are expected to participate in research and see clients. It is more important to be organized and structure time well."

In spite of the increased difficulty of the work and the increased time commitment, almost all of the graduate students we surveyed thought that graduate school was much more rewarding than college.

As Cindy Chappell, who is earning an Ed.D. in educational foundations at the University of Cincinnati, puts it, "[Graduate school] is so much better than undergrad. You get to focus on what you are interested in and you can make each and every course contribute to your goals. I feel much more connected to my school and department—like I am part of it rather than a consumer."

For some students, the transition to graduate school from college was more difficult because of a dramatic change in their living circumstances. For example, Stephanie Muntone went from a small-town campus in Ohio to a large, urban university when she enrolled at New York University. "The biggest difference between college and grad school was that I was in a big city instead of a little town in Ohio. NYU was such a big university, and Oberlin was so small. Any time there were questions about things, it was a terrible hassle to get ahold of the person who had your paperwork..." Muntone continues, "In New York, I lived in an apartment, not a dorm. Your fellow students were not necessarily your social circle. There was a social circle in the department, but it did not necessarily extend to your personal social life." Heather Helms-Erikson, a Ph.D. candidate in human development and family studies at Penn State, had a similar experience when she went from Messiah College, a small school in Grantham, Pennsylvania, to the University of Maryland for a master's degree in marriage and family therapy. "I moved from a small town to a city," she recalls. "There was definitely culture shock going from a small school where everyone knows you to a large university where no one says hello."

For international students, adjusting to the academic differences between their own countries and the United States is often easier than adjusting to a foreign language and the American way of life, far from family and home. Luis De la Cruz, who earned his bachelor's degree in civil engineering from the Universidad Iberoamericana in Mexico City, found that getting used to the English language and the American lifestyle took some time. "Language was the most difficult adjustment, even with my 600 TOEFL score," says De la Cruz, who is earning an M.B.A. at Worcester Polytechnic Institute in Massachusetts. He recalls, "I also had to get used to the environment...Living far from my friends and family and in a different environment are the worst things about graduate school."

> "Graduate school is much more demanding than college. You should be enrolled only if you are serious about it; otherwise it is a waste of money and time."

"The big difference for me was being on my own in a foreign country rather than being with my family in my own country," says an Italian woman who earned a Ph.D. in Italian literature from Northwestern University. "The system [in Italy] was quite different," she continues. "At the University of Rome, I was part of a very large group of undergraduates majoring in English, so nobody knew if I attended classes or not. In graduate school, you get a lot of personal attention. In addition, the exam system was quite different—all written exams instead of oral exams, on fixed dates. Still, I did not find this hard to adjust to, except for the style of life."

From Work to Graduate School

For students who have been in the work force for a few years—or decades—the transition to graduate school involves an additional set of issues. Not only do they have to contend with the academic rigor and increased workload common to all graduate students, but those who have done well professionally have to accustom themselves to a sense of diminished prestige. "I had been in the work force for ten years before going back to school," says Tom Fuchs, who is earning a Psy.D. at the California School of Professional Psychology. "At first it was difficult to feel like I was starting back at the bottom and didn't know anything. Now in my fourth year, that has disappeared." Renee Lantz, a Ph.D. candidate in fire protection engineering at Worcester Polytechnic Institute, agrees that having the low status of a student was a difficult adjustment. "It was hard to become such an underling again," she comments, "after years of professional experience."

Students who have been out of school for a long time are often self-confident professionals, but the idea of doing research, writing papers, and taking exams makes them very nervous because it's been years since they have had to do these things. According to Jay Sokolovsky, Professor of Anthropology at the University of South Florida, "Older students are at a disadvantage at first because they are out of the habit of writing, synthesizing, and taking exams." Bob Connelly agrees. "Going in, I had a lot of insecurity and self-doubt," recalls Connelly, who is Superintendent of Schools for Delaware Township, New Jersey. "Even though Seton Hall had accepted me [into their executive doctoral program in educational administration], I wasn't sure I could do it. I later found out that these feelings were common," says Connelly. "I was also concerned about my age, but to my surprise I found that most of the students were between 48 and 52 years old. Since we were of the same generation, that helped bond us."

Unlike Connelly, most older graduate students find themselves in programs with students—and some professors—younger than themselves. Leslie Nelman, who is earning a master's degree in translation and interpretation from the Monterey Institute of International Studies in California after twenty-two years in the business world, comments, "Perhaps the most interesting adjustment is having classmates half my age, as well as being older than many of the professors." Andrea Edwards Myers, who had not taken a college course in twenty-five years when she enrolled in the master's degree program in public communications at the College of St. Rose in Albany, New York, says, "Because of my age, I have made great friends with both the students and the faculty."

In addition to dealing with issues related to prestige and age, students who have grown accustomed to having free time when not at work find it hard to give that up. "I had been out of college for five years when I started my M.S.W. program, so I had to adjust from working full-time to being a full-time student again. The hardest part of that adjustment was giving up a lot of the free time that I used to enjoy when I was working," comments Felecia Bartow, a student at Washington University in St. Louis. "Depending upon one's job, many people can leave their work behind them at the end of the day. However, in graduate school, there is always something that you could or should be doing, and it is harder to justify spending time on nonacademic activities."

Students with family commitments have even more demands on their time. "I still find having to do homework or studying for an exam difficult because I got used to leaving work at work and having my own time when at home," says Tom Fuchs. "Now I make sure I reserve time for my wife and children, but unfortunately there is always some awareness of the need to get school work done."

However, there are compensations for the older student with work and family commitments. Tom Fuchs explains the benefits of being a mature student. "I really enjoy being in school after working for awhile. I appreciate...the process of learning so much more now than I did when I was in college or in law school right after college. Plus, I have a lot more life experience, so I think that makes the studying of psychology even richer for me than for someone just out of college." J. W. Viers, Director of Graduate Studies for the chemistry department at Virginia Tech, characterizes mature students as "usually more serious. They've seen what life is like on the outside with a B.A."

THE LIFE OF A GRADUATE STUDENT

One word sums up the life of a typical graduate student—busy. Graduate students have courses to take, research to do, papers to write, projects to present, and exams for which they must study. Often they work as well, then go home to families who would like some of their time and attention. One graduate student in library and information science who works full-time, goes to school part-time, and has a husband and young daughter guessed that her personal free time was less than 5 percent—and she thought that was a generous estimate.

Students who attend graduate school full-time don't have much personal time, either. "Depending upon the rigor of individual courses in any given semester, being in grad school full-time is a constant juggling act of one's time and energy—reading, writing papers, internship activities, research, etc.," says Felecia Bartow. "Personally, I do not find that I have much (if any) extra time for nonacademic activities or socializing with friends and colleagues, except during semester breaks."

Cindy Liutkus finds that her experience of full-time graduate study is similar. "Daily graduate student life entails laboratory work, attending classes, teaching laboratories, literature searching, and meeting with guest speakers...and that's all before lunch," explains Liutkus. "After work, there is often time to meet up with friends, but people are very understanding that work comes first."

Because there is so much to do, graduate students find that time management is essential to their success. "The most difficult aspect of grad school (like many other things in life) is time management—trying to get many things done at once and constantly resetting priorities," says Leslie Nelman. "The best part comes when you have succeeded at

One graduate student in library and information science who works full-time, goes to school part-time, and has a husband and young daughter guessed that her personal free time was less than 5 percent—and she thought that was a generous estimate.

this juggling act and realize how much you have accomplished by stretching yourself and doing more than you thought you could."

Like Nelman, Cindy Chappell thinks that time management is critical to a graduate student's ability to cope with all the demands on his or her time. "[Graduate school] is like a 24-hour job. There is always something waiting to be done, and it is hard to relax because you know you should be doing something else. Time management skills are very important to cultivate; if you can do this well, you can enjoy your 'time off,'" says Chappell. "My friends and family find it difficult to understand the stress that I am under. I think they think that since I am working at home (so to speak) that my work is easy..." Chappell thinks there is a bright side to the pressures of graduate school. "On the other side of the coin, I feel that the work I am doing has more value than a typical job, so the extra time and stress are worth it. Although I occasionally yearn for a typical 8 to 5 job that you leave at the office, I know that what I am doing has importance beyond putting food on the table."

Some graduate students find it difficult to keep up with all the things they have to do, especially when they are unfamiliar with the pace of graduate school. "The most important advice...is not to fall behind. If you are not on the ball from day one, it will just get worse. I fell behind first semester my first year and had a really tough time getting back on track," says Naaz Qureshi, who is earning an M.B.A. at Cox School of Business at Southern Methodist University in Dallas. "However, the second semester I was ahead and it made all the difference, particularly while looking for an internship."

The Worst of Times...

For many students, trying to do too much in too little time is the worst aspect of graduate school. Bob Connelly, who earned an Ed.D. from Seton Hall University in New Jersey while working full-time, was enrolled in a cohort program in which a group of students starts at the same time and stays together while working toward the degree. He found that the pressure to keep up with the group eventually increased to the point that he thought he was going to fall behind. "I was determined to do the degree in two years. Balancing my course work, comprehensive exams, dissertation, and job became a monumental task. In August of the second year, I was coming unglued," recalls Connelly. "I had to prepare the final requirements for the four courses I had taken that July, take the comprehensives in late September, and prepare three chapters of my dissertation." Connelly turned to his family for help. "I talked about it with my wife—whether to extend the time needed for the degree or to become a hermit for a couple of months and go for it. We decided I should go for it." With his wife's help and understanding, Connelly was able to concentrate on his studies and complete the degree with the rest of his cohort.

For other students, the worst part of graduate student life is not the stress of having too much to do, but the relative poverty. "The worst thing about graduate school is that it means that you have to pretty much be poor for a couple more years," says Kimani Toussaint. "Most of your peers that you went to undergraduate school with will be out there earning a lot of money, while you—if you're lucky—will be living off a small monthly stipend." Jennifer Cheavens agrees with Toussaint's assessment. "The worst thing is that you are very poor and probably going into debt," she says.

Other students worry about the future, especially if they are in fields with uncertain employment prospects. "The worst thing is thinking about how I am going to take this learning to make a living," says Tom Fuchs. "The market for psychologists is very tight and in a great state of flux because of the battles with managed health care."

...And the Best of Times

Yet for most graduate students, it doesn't much matter that they are feeling stress because they have too much to do, too little money, or too many worries about the future. There's an exhilaration associated with working toward your dream that gets you through all that. As Heather Helms-Erikson says about graduate school, "I love it. I love being surrounded by learning—not just in classes but with my peers, in clinical work, and in research. I love being surrounded by other people who are interested in learning."

Being a part of a community of scholars and students is one of the most positive aspects of graduate school for many students. "The best thing about grad school is the people," claims Jennifer Cheavens. "The professors are interested in your learning and the progress you are making. The students..have similar interests and you spend so much time around them that you become really close." She continues, "You are surrounded by people (both faculty members and students) who are thinking about things that interest you in new and different ways. The opportunity to learn and think in new ways is always encouraged."

Felecia Bartow agrees. "The best part about grad school is feeling intellectually challenged, being introduced to new and exciting information, and being part of a community of people who are interested in learning and exchanging ideas," she says.

According to a Ph.D. candidate in physics at Harvard, the best thing about graduate school is "being in an academic environment, relatively sheltered from the 'real world' and full of people whose main interest is in exploring ideas." As Neill Kipp, a Ph.D. candidate in computer science at Virginia Tech, puts it, "...a conversation about the postmodern philosophy of self-organizing systems is not something you overhear at Dilbert's water cooler."

For other students, the greatest pleasures of graduate school come from the work itself. "The best thing about graduate school is that it really is more about learning than it is about grades," says Kimani Toussaint. "Everyone is pretty much expected to do well. The approach that the students take, and the professors, is that everyone is in graduate school to learn. In the case of the engineering sciences, graduate school is a great opportunity to work on various research projects that could be considered on the cutting-edge of science." Another engineering student, Mike Ogburn, who is earning a master's degree in mechanical engineering at Virginia Tech, explains, "The best thing about graduate school is having a chance to focus on areas of work I enjoy. There is more continuity in my work now, and I am involved with industry in developing fuel-cell powered vehicles. Basically, I'm getting paid to play."

The joy that arises from their work is a benefit felt by graduate students who have found their niche. "My adviser had written a grant that provided expenses for her graduate students to accompany her to Africa, so in addition to working with her on her research topics, I had

The best thing about graduate school is that it really is more about learning than it is about grades.

the opportunity to complete my own work for my thesis. It was an incredible experience..." says Cindy Liutkus. "There is no substitute for working in the field, and there were many times when I would stop and look around at the African savanna and marvel at where I was and the opportunity I had been given."

For students pursuing degrees relating to their careers, what they learn in graduate school can give them a new perspective on their professions. For example, after twenty-three years in education and having achieved the highest position in his field—superintendent—Bob Connelly entered the executive Ed.D. program at Seton Hall. "I had not read the literature for a long time, and now I had to read the literature," says Connelly. "It was nice to get a conceptual framework for things I'd been doing intuitively. In addition, I was forced to write more and became a better writer."

For many students, the best thing about graduate school is its potential to change your life. According to Jean Godby, who is earning a Ph.D. in linguistics at Ohio State, "You make friends for life. You also develop values that shape the rest of your life. As a result of my graduate school experience, I know I have inner resources to solve problems, I have deep aesthetic values, and I am not caught up in the overheated American consumer culture."

Nestor Montilla also sees graduate education as the key to his future. "When I moved to the U.S.A., my window of opportunities was as narrow as the hole of a needle," says Montilla. "I entered college, earned my first A.A.S. degree, then a B.A. After that, I realized that a graduate degree would expand that window of opportunities even further. Today, I am about to earn a master's degree. My academic success opens many doors that were closed before."

THE BENEFITS OF HINDSIGHT

When we asked students what they would have done differently if they had known when they started their graduate education what they know today, a surprising number said, "Nothing." Despite the mistakes they may have made along the way, in general, most students felt they had gotten the education that was right for them.

However, a few students did express regrets about the direction their education had taken. One student felt that her initial decision to pursue a master's degree in library and information science was a mistake. "I now realize how very much I like to share my professional knowledge with others. If I were to do it over again, I would have only considered pursuing a Ph.D. and only if I was offered a substantial scholarship," she says. "The decision to pursue a Ph.D. program or master's-level program is best made at the outset for both financial and psychological reasons." As you recall from Chapter 2, deciding whether to pursue a master's or doctoral degree is one of the first questions you need to answer when you first consider graduate education.

A student who chose her graduate program because it accepted late applications now regrets the complications that ensued because she had not been more selective. "I would probably try to go to a university where there would be professors whose research interests matched mine," she explains. "What happened with me was that I basically had to do my dissertation on my own, because nobody could really follow me at my institution. I had to rely on external readers, which is always a pain in terms of communication, and really be very independent." Another woman also wished she had been more discriminating when applying to programs. "I think I should have spent more time applying to schools. I applied to the one school I knew for sure I'd get into," she says. "I think I should have challenged myself a little more."

Kim Foreman, a health-care administrator who started her graduate work seventeen years after graduating from college, regrets waiting so long. "If I had to do it over again...I would have started sooner," she explains. "It's never too late to learn and now it's so easy and accessible, but I think it would have enhanced my work performance if I had started my graduate program earlier." This sentiment was echoed by several of the older students, yet when they were pressed, most acknowledged that the main reason they had waited so long was that they simply had not been ready to resume their educations when they were younger. The primary reason they now wished that they had done their graduate work when they were in their twenties is that they felt it would have been easier if they had done so before having work and family commitments that competed for their time and attention. Despite the difficulties of earning an advanced degree while working and caring for a family, these students still felt their graduate educations were worth it. "After twenty-five years in education, I'm recharged," says Bob Connelly. "I'm even teaching a course as an adjunct, something that would not have been possible otherwise."

A doctoral candidate in a professional degree program regrets his indebtedness. "It would have been great to have been able to go full-time without needing to work. But the cost of dealing with student loans later is too high to not work. I did take some loans in the first year when I went to school full-time and worked part-time, but I wish I hadn't felt that was necessary," he explains.

Finally, some students wish they had planned their studies better and gotten to work sooner once they arrived on campus. One student, who regrets that she did not plan her course work efficiently, explains, "If I had to do anything differently, I would plan out my curriculum more precisely. As it turns out, I will be taking classes into the second semester of my second year, whereas most students either take only one class or have completely finished their course work by that time." Another student regrets getting off to a slow start at the beginning of his doctoral program. "I would have started being serious with my literature review as soon as I arrived: note cards, computer files, every spare moment in the library or on the Internet reading—to find out firsthand what problems were waiting to be solved and what blind alleys people have gone down," he explains. "If I had, maybe I could have graduated by now!"

Still, the majority of students were satisfied with their graduate educations—with the programs they chose, the work they did, and the degree they earned. Cindy Chappell sums up her experience: "I've made some mistakes along the way, such as taking too much time with each degree, but I have benefited from the same mistakes as well. It's difficult for me to separate the pluses from the minuses. I have been quite successful thus far, so I would hesitate to change anything...I have followed my gut even when authority figures have told me I was pursuing the wrong things, and I have triumphed—as much as one can in graduate school!"

Perhaps the best, most succinct words of advice are those of Cindy Liutkus: "Do your homework—find out all there is to know about the schools to which you want to apply: who your adviser would be, what work you'd be doing, how big the department is, what the cost of living is, and so on. Weigh all of your options—ask yourself what criteria are most important to you and rank your choices accordingly. Be true to yourself—remember that you are the one applying to graduate school. Make your decisions based on what you feel...When you are comfortable with your decisions, the rest will fall into place."

Worksheets

TIMETABLE

Here is a sample timetable for applying to a program whose application deadline is between January and March for enrollment in the following August or September. Check your applications for exact deadlines and modify this schedule accordingly. All dates are approximate.

Month	Tasks	Task Done
February	Do self-assessment. Register for standardized admissions test. Prepare for test.	
March	Start doing research on programs. Continue preparing for test.	
April	Continue research on programs. Take standardized admission test.	
May	Continue research on programs. Start research on external fellowships and scholarships.	
June	Compile preliminary list of programs. Compile preliminary list of external fellowships and scholarships.	
July	Narrow list of programs. Narrow list of fellowships and scholarships. Prepare for retaking standardized test, if necessary.	
August	Register to retake standardized test and continue preparing. Begin requesting applications from programs and fellowship organizations. Start thinking about and outlining personal essay.	
September	Request letters of recommendation. Draft personal essay. Continue preparing to retake standardized test. Register for required subject area test and start preparing.	

Appendix 1

Game Plan for Getting into Graduate School

Month	Tasks	Task Done
October	Retake standardized admission test, if necessary. Get feedback on personal essay. Continue preparing for subject area test. Begin filling out application forms.	
November	Take subject area test, if required. Arrange for official transcripts to be sent out by registrar(s). Finish personal essay. Follow up on letters of recommendation. Continue working on application forms.	
December	Assemble and copy completed applications. Start submitting applications.	
January	Request and prepare FAFSA, if applying for need-based aid. Finish submitting applications.	
February	Follow up on status of applications.	
March	Evaluate offers of acceptance. Visit programs.	
April	Inform programs of your decision.	

SELF-ASSESSMENT WORKSHEET

GOALS

What are your long-term professional goals? What would you like to be doing in five to ten years?

_____

_____

_____

_____

_____

Will a graduate degree help you achieve these goals? If so, which degree and in what field?

_____

_____

FIELD OF STUDY

Can you imagine spending most of your time on this subject for several years of graduate school and then for the rest of your life in related professional work?

_____

_____

NOW OR LATER?

What are the pros and cons of going to graduate school straight from college?

_____

_____

_____

_____

What are the pros and cons of working for a few years before graduate school?

_____

_____

_____

_____

YOUR QUALIFICATIONS

What academic and professional qualifications will enable you to pursue this degree?

_____

_____

_____

_____

If you lack some qualifications, what must you do to make them up?

_____

_____

_____

_____

YOUR PERSONAL CHARACTERISTICS

Evaluate your ability to do the kind of academic work you will be doing in graduate school-reading, research, synthesizing, and writing.

_____

_____

_____

_____

Evaluate yourself in terms of the motivation, self-discipline, self-confidence, interpersonal skills, and persistence needed to earn a graduate degree.

_____

_____

_____

_____

_____

_____

Are you willing to commit the time, effort, and personal and financial resources that pursuing a graduate degree requires?

_____

_____

PROGRAM SELECTION CRITERIA WORKSHEET

Criteria	Program 1	Program 2	Program 3
Faculty			
Program reputation			
Program/ university accreditation			
Academic issues			
Your own qualifications			
Availability of internships			
Placement of graduates			
Size			
Diversity			
Full-time or part-time			
On-campus or distance learning			
Average time to complete degree			
Location			

Game Plan for Getting into Graduate School   www.petersons.com

Criteria	Program 1	Program 2	Program 3
Cost of attendance			
Likelihood of getting funding			
University environment			
Community environment			
Other factors			
Your overall assessment (1=low; 10=high)			

COST OF ATTENDANCE/EXPENSE BUDGET WORKSHEET

Typical Expenses and Income of a Graduate Student

Personal Costs	Month	Year
Housing	_____	_____
Food	_____	_____
Utilities	_____	_____
Telephone	_____	_____
Clothing	_____	_____
Laundry/dry cleaning	_____	_____
Entertainment	_____	_____
Personal expenses	_____	_____
Transportation	_____	_____
Insurance	_____	_____
Medical expenses	_____	_____
Child care (if applicable)	_____	_____
Credit cards	_____	_____
Other indebtedness	_____	_____
Total	_____	_____

School-Related Costs: A Projection Based on Three Possible Choices

Graduate Schools	1._____	2._____	3._____
Costs			
Tuition	_____	_____	_____
Fees	_____	_____	_____
Books and supplies	_____	_____	_____
Travel	_____	_____	_____
Other	_____	_____	_____
	_____	_____	_____
Total for one year	_____	_____	_____
Sources of Funds			
Savings	_____	_____	_____
Earnings, one year	_____	_____	_____
Parent's contribution	_____	_____	_____
Spouse's contribution	_____	_____	_____
Scholarships	_____	_____	_____
Fellowships	_____	_____	_____
Federal and state aid administered by school	_____	_____	_____
Loans	_____	_____	_____
Veteran's benefits	_____	_____	_____
Social Security benefits	_____	_____	_____
Stocks, bonds	_____	_____	_____
Other resources	_____	_____	_____
Total available	_____	_____	_____

Reprinted with permission from Patricia McWade, *Financing Graduate School*, Peterson's, 1996, pp. 19-20.

Resources

CHAPTER 1: INTRODUCTION

Council of Graduate Schools
One Dupont Circle, NW
Washington, D.C. 20036-1173
Phone: 202-223-3791
Web site: http://www.cgsnet.org

Chronicle of Higher Education
1255 23d Street, NW
Washington, D.C. 20037
Phone: 202-466-1000
E-mail: circulation@chronicle.com
Web site: http://www.chronicle.com

National Library of Education
U.S. Department of Education
400 Maryland Avenue, SW
Washington, D.C. 20202
Phone: 800-424-1616 (toll-free)
E-mail: library@inet.ed.gov
Web site: http://www.nces.ed.gov/NLE

CHAPTER 2: ASSESSING YOURSELF

National Board for Certified Counselors
3 Terrace Way, Suite D
Greensboro, North Carolina 27403-3660
Phone: 800-398-5389 (toll-free)
E-mail: nbcc@nbcc.org
Web site: http://www.nbcc.org

Appendix 2

CHAPTER 3: LOCATING INFORMATION

Print Media

General Guidance

Finkle, Jane, ed. *Graduate School: The Best Resources to Help You Choose, Get In, and Pay*. Seattle: Resource Pathways, 1998. A guidebook that includes reviews of sources of information, including print, Internet, and software, on various aspects of graduate school.

Specific Fields of Study

Brown, Sanford J., M.D. *Getting Into Medical School: The Premedical Student's Guidebook*, 8th ed. Barron's, 1997.

Byrne, John A. Business Week's Guide to the Best Business Schools. New York: McGraw-Hill, 1997.

Clark, Robert, and John Palatella. *Real Guide to Graduate School: What You Better Know Before You Choose Humanities and Social Science*. Linguafranca Books, 1997.

Coleman, Ron. *Prelaw Companion: What Law School Grads Wish They Knew Before They Started*. Princeton Review, 1996.

Insider's Guide to Medical School. Princeton, N.J.: Peterson's, 1999.

Jewell, C. S. *Game Plan for Getting into Medical School*. Princeton, N.J.: Peterson's, 2000.

Kornegay, Michele F. *Game Plan for Getting into Business School*. Princeton, N.J.: Peterson's, 2000.

Law School Admissions Council. *Thinking About Law School: A Minority Guide*. Free booklet available from the LSAC (http://www.lsac.org or 215-968-1001).

Montauk, Richard. *How to Get Into the Top M.B.A. Programs*. Englewood Cliffs, N.J.: Prentice-Hall, 1997.

Reyes, Jesus, A. M., A.C.S.W. *The Guide to Selecting and Applying to M.S.W. Programs*. In addition to giving advice, lists accredited programs in the United States.

Weaver, Bill. *Game Plan for Getting into Law School*. Princeton, N.J.: Peterson's, 2000.

Directories

International Student Handbook of U.S. Colleges, 11th ed. College Board, 1998.

Law School Admissions Council. *Official Guide to U.S. Law Schools.* New York: Broadway Books, 1998. This directory is of particular interest to minority students because it has a long chapter on opportunities in law, including data on minority representation in school faculties and student bodies.

Peterson's Distance Learning Programs 2000. Princeton, N.J.: Peterson's, 2000.

Peterson's Guide to Graduate and Professional Programs, Volumes 1-6. Princeton, N.J.: Peterson's, published annually. This is the set of directories with information on virtually every single graduate program. It is available in libraries, or you can buy single volumes in bookstores or directly from Peterson's; prices range from $31.96 to $39.96 per volume (http://www.petersons.com or 800-225-0261).

Peterson's Law Schools 1999. Princeton, N.J.: Peterson's, 1999.

Peterson's MBA Programs 2000. Princeton, N.J.: Peterson's, 2000. An easy-to-use and thorough directory of 900 business school programs.

Peterson's Professional Degree Programs in the Visual and Performing Arts, 1998. Princeton, N.J.: Peterson's, 1998. Besides describing more than 1,000 programs in studio art, design, dance, music, and theater, this directory offers tips on preparing portfolios and tapes and preparing for auditions.

Peterson's U.S. and Canadian Medical Schools 1999. Princeton, N.J.: Peterson's, 1999. Profiles all 159 accredited medical schools.

Peterson's/U-Wire Quick Focus Grad Series. A series of one-volume print directories with CD-ROMs that include in-depth profiles of selected institutions and GRE test-prep software. Volumes include Graduate Schools; Arts, Humanities, and Archaeology; Biology, Health, and Agricultural Sciences; Education; Engineering, Computer Science, and Information Studies; Physical Sciences, Mathematics, and Environmental Sciences; and Social Sciences and Social Work. Princeton, N.J.: Peterson's, 1999.

Internet Resources

General Information and Fields of Study

Association for Support of Graduate Students (http://www.asgs.org). Lots of information of interest to graduate students.

Boston College's Online Law School Locator (http://www.bc.edu:80/bc_org/svp/carct/matrix.html). Match your LSAT scores and GPA with those of the average first-year student at various schools to find a range of schools.

Council of Graduate Schools (http://www.cgsnet.org). Of particular interest is the Student Page, which has links to information of interest to graduate students.

Internet Legal Resource Guide (http://www.ilrg.com). Lots of onsite information as well as links to hundreds of law-related sites.

Peterson's (http://www.petersons.com). Lots of articles about various aspects of graduate schools plus access to the online searchable databases.

Directories

GradSchools.com (http://www.gradschools.com). Search by field of study, then region.

Peterson's Guides (http://www.petersons.com). Online access to information on more than 35,000 programs in all fields of study, both academic and professional, distilled from Peterson's six-volume directory of graduate programs. Sophisticated search capabilities.

Study in the USA (http://www.studyusa.com). First stop for international students.

CHAPTER 4: SELECTING PROGRAMS

Rankings

Research-Doctorate Programs in the United States: Continuity and Change. Washington, D.C.: National Academy Press, 1995.

Student Guide to Research-Doctorate Programs. Washington, D.C.: National Research Council, 1996. A condensed version of Research-Doctorate Programs in the United States: Continuity and Change.

Regional Accrediting Agencies

Middle States Association of Colleges and Schools
3624 Market Street
Philadelphia, Pennsylvania 19104-2680
Phone: 215-662-5606
Web site: http://www.msache.org
Accredits institutions in Delaware, District of Columbia, Maryland, New Jersey, New York, Pennsylvania, Puerto Rico, and the Virgin Islands.

New England Association of Schools and Colleges
209 Burlington Road
Bedford, Massachusetts 01730-1433
Phone: 781-271-0022
Web site: http://www.neasc.org
Accredits institutions in Connecticut, Maine, Massachusetts, New Hampshire, Rhode Island, and Vermont.

North Central Association of Colleges and Schools
30 North LaSalle, Suite 2400
Chicago, Illinois 60602-2504
Phone: 800-621-7440 (toll-free)
E-mail: info@ncacihe.org
Web site: http://www.ncacihe.org
Accredits institutions in Arizona, Arkansas, Colorado, Illinois, Indiana, Iowa, Kansas, Michigan, Minnesota, Missouri, Nebraska, New Mexico, North Dakota, Ohio, Oklahoma, South Dakota, West Virginia, Wisconsin, and Wyoming.

Northwest Association of Schools and Colleges
1910 University Drive
Boise, Idaho 83725-1060
Phone: 208-334-3210
Web site: http://www2.idbsu.edu/nasc
Accredits institutions in Alaska, Idaho, Montana, Nevada, Oregon, Utah, and Washington.

Southern Association of Colleges and Schools
1866 Southern Lane

Decatur, Georgia 30033-4097
Phone: 404-679-4500
Web site: http://www.sacscoc.org
Accredits institutions in Alabama, Florida, Georgia, Kentucky, Louisiana, Mississippi, North Carolina, South Carolina, Tennessee, Texas, and Virginia.

Western Association of Schools and Colleges
985 Atlantic Avenue, Suite 100
Alameda, California 94501
Phone: 510-632-5000
Web site: http://www.wascweb.org
Accredits institutions in California, Guam, and Hawaii.

Other Institutional Accrediting Agencies

Accrediting Council for Independent Colleges and Schools
750 First Street, NE, Suite 980
Washington, D.C. 20002-4241
Phone: 202-842-2593
E-mail: info@acics.org
Web site: http://www.acics.org

Distance Education and Training Council
1601 Eighteenth Street, NW
Washington, D.C. 20009-2529
Phone: 202-234-5100
E-mail: detc@detc.org
Web site: http://www.detc.org

Specialized Accrediting Agencies

In addition to the accrediting agencies listed above, there are specialized agencies that accredit programs and institutions in the following fields: acupuncture, art and design, chiropractic, clinical laboratory science, dance, dentistry, education, engineering, environment, forestry, health services administration, interior design, journalism and mass communications, landscape architecture, law, library, marriage and family therapy, medical illustration, medicine, music, naturopathic medicine, nurse anesthesia, nurse midwifery, nursing, occupational therapy, optometry, osteopathic medicine, pastoral education, pharmacy, physical therapy, planning, podiatric medicine, psychology and counseling, public affairs and administration, public health, rabbinical and Talmudic education, rehabilitation education, social work, speech-language pathology and audiology, theater, theology, and veterinary medicine.

To find the names and contact information for these accrediting agencies, consult the front matter of *Peterson's Guide to Graduate and Professional Programs, volume 1,* or *Peterson's/U-Wire Graduate Schools in the U.S., 1999* (Quick Focus Grad Series).

CHAPTER 5: TAKING GRADUATE ADMISSIONS TESTS

GREs

For information about the GREs, contact the Educational Testing Service:

GRE-ETS
P.O. Box 6000
Princeton, New Jersey 08541-6000
Phone: 609-771-7670
E-mail: gre-info@ets.org
Web site (GRE Online): http://www.gre.org

You can obtain a copy of the 1999-2000 GRE Information and Registration Bulletin by phoning ETS or by downloading it from the Web site. To schedule an appointment to take the General Test or Writing Test in the United States, Puerto Rico, or Canada, call 800-GRE-CALL (toll-free). International students should check the Bulletin or the Web site for a list of regional registration sites. To register for a Subject Test, use the paper form in the Bulletin or sign up on the Web site.

The Web site also offers a lot of other material that can be downloaded: practice tests, descriptions of the subject area tests, and preparation software.

GRE Big Book. Order from ETS at http://www.gre.org.

GRE Powerprep Software. Includes test preparation for both the General Test and the Writing Assessment. Can be downloaded for $45 from http://www.gre.org.

Peterson's GRE CAT Success. A test preparation book that provides strategies, review and practice for the GRE CAT. Includes free access to Peterson's online simulated GRE CAT. Princeton, N.J.: Peterson's, 2000.

Practice Books for Subject Area Tests. Order from http://www.gre.org.

MAT

The Psychological Corporation
555 Academic Court
San Antonio, Texas 78204
Phone: 800-622-3231 (toll-free)
Web site: http://www.tpcweb.com/mat

GMAT

GMAT
Distribution and Receiving Center
225 Phillips Boulevard
Ewing, New Jersey 08628-7435
Phone: 609-771-7330
E-mail: gmat@ets.org
Web site (MBA Explorer): http://www.gmat.org

Peterson's GMAT CAT Success. A test preparation book that provides strategies, review and practice for the GMAT CAT. Includes free access to Peterson's online simulated GRE CAT. Princeton, N.J.: Peterson's, 2000.

LSAT

LSAT
Law School Admissions Council

Newtown, Pennsylvania 18940
Phone: 215-968-1001
E-mail: LSACinfo@lsac.org
Web site: http://www.lsac.org

Peterson's LSAT Success. Princeton, N.J.: Peterson's, 2000.

MCAT

MCAT Program Office
P.O. Box 4056
Iowa City, Iowa 52243
Phone: 319-337-1357
E-mail: mcat@aamc.org
Web site: http://www.aamc.org

Ferdinand, Brett L. *The Gold Standard MCAT: The Ultimate Comprehensive Science Review.* Princeton, N.J.: Peterson's, 1998.
Peterson's MCAT Success. Princeton, N.J.: Peterson's, 1999.

TOEFL and TSE

Information on both the TOEFL and the TSE can be obtained from
the Educational Testing Service:

TOEFL
P.O. Box 6151
Princeton, New Jersey 08541-6151
Phone: 609-771-7100
E-mail: toefl@ets.org
Web site: http://toefl.org

Rogers, Bruce. *TOEFL Practice Tests 2000.* Princeton, N.J.: Peterson's,
2000. Can be purchased with audiocassettes to prepare for the
listening section.
Rogers, Bruce. *TOEFL Success 1999.* Princeton, N.J.: Peterson's, 1999.
Can be purchased with audiocassettes to prepare for the listening section.

CHAPTER 6: APPLYING

Business School

GradAdvantage
E-mail: gradadv@ets.org
Web site: http://www.gradadvantage.org

Law School

Law School Data Assembly Service
Box 2000-M
Newtown, Pennsylvania 18940-0993
Phone: 215-968-1001
E-mail: LSACinfo@lsac.org
Web site: http://www.lasc.org

Medical School

American Medical College Application Services
2501 M Street, NW
Washington, DC 20037-1300
Phone: 202-828-0600
E-mail: amcas@aamc.org
Web site: http://www.aamc.org

CHAPTER 7: WRITING A GOOD PERSONAL ESSAY

Curry, Boykin, and Brian Kasbar. *Essays That Worked for Business School: 35 Essays from Successful Applications to the Nation's Top Business Schools.* New York: Fawcett Columbine, 1987.

Stelzer, Richard J. *How to Write a Winning Personal Statement for Graduate and Professional School, 3d ed.* Princeton, N.J.: Peterson's, 1997. Lots of suggestions, both from the author and admissions representatives of graduate and professional schools, along with many sample essays.

CHAPTER 8: PAYING

General Information

Financial Aid Information Page (http://www.finaid.org). The best place to start an Internet search for financial aid information.

McWade, Patricia. *Financing Graduate School*. Princeton, N.J.: Peterson's, 1996. The best, most detailed treatment of financial aid for graduate students, written by the Dean of Student Financial Services at Georgetown University.

National Association of Student Financial Aid Administrators (http://www.nasfaa.org). Lots of essays explain various aspects of financial aid, including educational tax credits.

State Residency

Todd, Daryl F., Jr. *How to Cut Tuition: The Complete Guide to In-State Tuition*. Linwood, N.J.: Atlantic Educational Publishing, 1997.

Fellowships

AJR Newslink (http://www.newslink.org). Awards, grants, and scholarships for journalism students.

Annual Register of Grant Support: A Directory of Funding Sources. Wilmette, Ill.: National Register Publishing Company.

Corporate Foundation Profiles. New York: Foundation Center, 1999 (http://www.fdncenter.org or 212-620-4230).

FastWeb (http://www.fastweb.com). The best of the online searchable databases of scholarships and fellowships.

National Science Foundation (http://www.nsf.gov/home/students). Of interest to students in the sciences. About 1,000 three-year fellowships are awarded annually.

Peterson's Grants for Graduate and Postdoctoral Study, 5th ed. Compiled by the University of Massachusetts, Amherst. Princeton, N.J.: Peterson's, 1998. More than 1,400 fellowships and other awards, indexed by field of study as well as special characteristics of the recipients (e.g., ethnic minority groups).

Schlachter, Gail Ann, and R. David Weber. *Money for Graduate Students in the Humanities*. Reference Service Press, 1998.

Schlachter, Gail Ann, and R. David Weber. *Money for Graduate Students in the Social Sciences*. Reference Service Press, 1998.

Cooperative Education

Re, Joseph M. *Earn and Learn*. Octameron Associates, 1997.

Federal Aid

U.S. Department of Education
400 Maryland Avenue, SW
Washington, D.C. 20202-0498
The Department of Education maintains a huge and useful Web site (http://www.ed.gov).

- For information on Student Financial Assistance Programs, including work study, Perkins Loans, Stafford Loans, and other federal aid, check http://www.ed.gov/offices/OSFAP/Students.
- For a copy of the 1999-2000 Student Financial Aid Handbook, go to http://www.ifap.ed.gov.
- For the FAFSA, go to FAFSA Online (http://www.FAFSA.ed.gov).

Or, you can call the Federal Student Aid Information Center at 800-4-FEDAID (toll-free).

Private Loans

Note that this is not an exhaustive list. Contact your university's financial aid office for other sources of loans.

Graduate School

American Express Alternative Loan. American Express/California Higher Education Loan Authority, 800-255-8374 (toll-free).

CollegeReserve Loan. USA Group, 800-538-8492 (toll-free) or http://www.usagroup.com.

EXCEL Loan. Nellie Mae, 888-2TUITION (toll-free) or http://www. nelliemae.org.

Graduate Access Loan. The Access Group, 800-282-1550 (toll-free) or http://www.accessgrp.org.

Signature Student Loan. Sallie Mae, 888-272-5543 (toll-free) or http:// www.salliemae.com.

Business School

Business Access Loan Program. The Access Group, 800-282-1550 (toll-free) or http://www.accessgrp.org.

M.B.A. Loans and the Tuition Loan Plan (TLP). Contact your school's financial aid office.

MBASHARE. New England Loan Marketing Association (Nellie Mae), 50 Braintree Hill Park, Suite 300, Braintree, MA 02184, 800-634-9308 (toll-free).

Law School

Law Access Loan. The Access Group, 800-282-1550 (toll-free) or http://www.accessgrp.org.

LawLoans. LawLoans customer service, 800-366-5626 (toll-free).

LawSHARE. New England Loan Marketing Association (Nellie Mae), 50 Braintree Hill Park, Suite 300, Braintree, MA 02184, 800-634-9308 (toll-free).

Medical School

AAMC MedLoans. Contact your school's financial aid office or the Association of American Medical Colleges, 2450 N Street, NW, Washington, DC 20037.

Medical Access Loans. The Access Group, 800-282-1550 (toll-free) or http://www.accessgrp.org.

MedSHARE. New England Loan Marketing Association (Nellie Mae), 50 Braintree Hill Park, Suite 300, Braintree, MA 02184, 800-634-9308 (toll-free).

Credit Reporting Agencies

It's a good idea to check your credit rating before applying for any loans. Call first to find out if there is a fee.

Experian
P.O. Box 9530
Allen, Texas 75013
Phone: 888-397-3742 (toll-free)

Equifax
P.O. Box 105873
Atlanta, Georgia 30348
Phone: 800-685-1111 (toll-free)

CSC Credit Services
Consumer Assistance Center
P.O. Box 674402
Houston, Texas 77267-4402
Phone: 800-759-5979 (toll-free)

Trans Union Corporation
P.O. Box 390
Springfield, Pennsylvania 19064-0390
Phone: 800-888-4213 (toll-free)

Women, Minority Students, Disabled Students, and Veterans

Bruce-Young, Doris M., and William C. Young. *Higher Education Money Book for Women and Minorities*. Young Enterprises International, 1997.

Minority and Women's Complete Scholarship Book; plus Scholarships for Religious Affiliations and People with Disabilities. Sourcebooks, 1998.

Olson, Elizabeth A. *Dollars for College (Women)*. Garrett Park Press, 1995.

Saludos Web Education Center (http://www.saludos.com). Internships and scholarships targeted to Hispanic Americans as well as those not considering race or ethnicity.

Schlachter, Gail Ann, and R. David Weber. *Financial Aid for African Americans*. Reference Service Press, 1997.

Schlachter, Gail Ann, and R. David Weber. *Financial Aid for the Disabled and Their Families*. Reference Service Press, 1998.

Schlachter, Gail Ann, and R. David Weber. *Financial Aid for Veterans, Military Personnel, and Their Dependents*. Reference Service Press, 1996.

Schlachter, Gail Ann. *Directory of Financial Aids for Women*. Reference Service Press, 1997.

International Students

Funding for U.S. Study-A Guide for International Students and Professionals and Financial Resources for International Study. New York: Institute of International Education (http://www.iiebooks.org).

Student Travel Catalogue. New York: Council on International Educational Exchange (http://www.ciee.org). This publication lists fellowships and explains the council's services for international students.

CSS Financial Aid Profile

Contact the College Scholarship Service at http://www.collegeboard.org or 305-829-9793.

Tax Issues

Tax Benefits for Higher Education. IRS Publication 970. Contact the Internal Revenue Service at http://www.irs.ustreas.gov/prod/forms_pubs/pubs/p970toc.htm or 800-829-3676 (toll-free).

CHAPTER 9: MAKING YOUR FINAL CHOICE

Resolution Regarding Graduate Scholars, Fellows, Trainees, and Assistants. The full text of the Council of Graduate Schools' resolution on the rules regarding acceptances and rejections of program offers can be downloaded from their Web site (http://www.cgsnet.org/publications/resolu.html). In addition, the gist of the resolution is explained on the site, and a list of signatory institutions is provided there.

CHAPTER 10: THE GRADUATE SCHOOL EXPERIENCE

Mitchell, Lesli. *The Ultimate Grad School Survival Guide*. Princeton, N.J.: Peterson's, 1996.

Peters, Robert L. *Getting What You Came For: the Smart Student's Guide to Earning a Master's or Ph.D.* New York: Noonday Press, 1997.

Association for the Support of Graduate Students
P.O. Box 4698
Incline Village, Nevada 89450-4698
Phone: 775-831-1399
E-mail: asgs@asgs.org
Web site: http://www.asgs.org

National Association of Graduate-Professional Students
825 Green Bay Road, Suite 270
Wilmette, Illinois 60091
Phone: 888-88-NAGPS (toll-free)
E-mail: nagps@netcom.com
Web site: http://www.nagps.org

NOTES

NOTES

NOTES

NOTES

NOTES

NOTES

Peterson's unplugged

graduate programs

distance learning

adult education

executive training

colleges

university

private secondary schools

internships and careers

study-abroad programs

financial aid scholarships

summer programs

Peterson's quality on every page!

For more than three decades, we've offered a complete selection of books to guide you in all of your educational endeavors. You can find our vast collection of titles at your local bookstore or online at **petersons.com**.

High school student headed for college?

Busy professional interested in distance learning?

Parent searching for the perfect private school or summer camp?

Human resource manager looking for executive education programs?

AOL Keyword: Petersons
Phone: 800-338-3282

Peterson's
Thomson Learning™